Nobody's Business

Nobody's Business
A taxi owner, a murder, and a secret
A memoir

Thabo Jijana

First published by Jacana Media (Pty) Ltd in 2014

10 Orange Street
Sunnyside
Auckland Park 2092
South Africa
+2711 628 3200
www.jacana.co.za

© Thabo Jijana, 2014

All rights reserved.

ISBN 978-1-4314-2029-2

Cover design by publicide
Set in Sabon 11/16pt
Printed and bound by Creda Communications
Job no. 002360

See a complete list of Jacana titles at www.jacana.co.za

To my father, an elegy

The tragedy is not that things are broken. The tragedy is that they are not mended again.
— Alan Paton

One

Anyone who has ever experienced a personal tragedy carries with them a vivid image of that moment just prior to their misfortune when everything seemed just right – that calm, unsuspecting moment before the storm swept in. Perhaps they were cradling a cup of tea at home, engrossed in their favourite soapie when the phone rang; or had gone to wake their child for breakfast only to discover that the bed had not been slept in ...

In my case, it was my winter school break in July 2003, and I had come to spend it with the family of my father's first cousin, my auntie Nolwandle, in the sleepy town of Peddie in the former Ciskei.

Each morning, the road outside auntie's township house swelled with the daily exodus of commuters – men in overalls and shiny boots with a pleased look in their eyes, women hurrying behind with tight *doeks* on their heads and handbags over their shoulders. *Da'bawo* Nolwandle, the eldest daughter of my grandfather's only brother, was one of these women.

Each morning I helped auntie's lastborn Monde* load her wares onto a rickety taxicab at the doorstep, and waved as the car carried her away to her vendor's stand in town. Back in the house our breakfast would be waiting for us, a plate of *amagwinya*, a piece of fried fish and a cup of black coffee. This was lavish fare for a boy of fifteen brought up on a frugal breakfast of sugared oatmeal or buttered bread with juice, and I intended to crow to my siblings about waking up to fish every day when I returned home. In the evenings, Monde and I would greet her when her taxi pulled up at the gate and help offload her merchandise: a metal bowl the size of a basin with bags of uncooked fish, bundles of fruit, and occasionally also bags of groceries.

I had last seen my sister and younger brother in late June, at the beginning of the holidays. How happy *da'bawo* Nolwandle had been to see us when my father drove us to her house from our village, the last of a group of villages to the south, known as eMazizini. As I stood at her gate, a little sad to see my siblings go, they smiled and waved goodbye, their hands poking out of the passenger door of our father's taxi van.

---

* Not his real name

After a couple of weeks I was getting used to "living in town", as I liked to boast to myself then. I had an incurable desire to be helpful, and felt proud that I had already proved useful around auntie's house. I had painted the inside of a brick flat and cut down to waist height the overgrown milkweed hedge that enclosed the courtyard.

Monde suffered from epileptic fits. Too much time in the sun always knocked him flat on the ground, motionless as a defeated boxer. So I spent much of my time doing what would have been his tasks, and then sitting with him in the shade, chatting about this or that. We didn't know each other well – I didn't know myself well – but if *da'bawo* Nolwandle had reason to be grateful for my presence, it was for the company I provided to Monde, who was a year or two older than me. Before I came along, while everyone else was at work or school, Monde spent most of his days with his elder sister and grandmother Magatyeni, who had to keep a strict eye that he didn't stay out in the sun too long. I had taken this load off their shoulders.

There were other livelier characters in this family that I had come to admire. Uncle Vuyani was a construction worker who lived with his family in eJamani, another of Peddie's townships, but came to visit us now and then, tipsy and full of witty stories in which the joke was often on himself. Mlungisi, the eldest of auntie's five children, was a municipal worker whose entire music collection amounted to a single Lionel Richie cassette. He played it nonstop after work in the late afternoons while reading *Soccer Laduma* or the *Daily Sun*. His generosity seemed boundless, as with many bachelor relatives. In the afternoon he would bring home a bag of oranges or a packet of ginger biscuits, earning him great favour among the children. In a way, Mlungisi was the man of the house, as auntie was divorced and took care of her mother, whom I called *makhulu* Magatyeni. But *bhut'* Langa, who was less than a decade older than me, was the cousin I had grown fondest of.

Although auntie's family was eleven in all, her RDP[1] house was tiny – a single room partitioned into a kitchen, lounge and two bedrooms by means of a long curtain, a wardrobe and a wall unit, respectively. So Langa slept in the house of a neighbour for whom he was housesitting, and I slept there with him.

I took a real liking to Langa. In his company I began to really look at myself now and pay attention to my own individual identity. This wasn't my first holiday with relatives, but living among auntie's family gave me a clearer sense of myself as a person. I realised now, with something close to pride, that as plain as I was, I enjoyed my solitude and was delighted to be working with my hands. Back in my father's household I lived among many adults who were used to doing things for themselves.

At night I would sit and listen as *bhut'* Langa talked and smoked cigarettes, sharing war stories about his romantic conquests in the local tavern, all of which fascinated me in the way the doings of adults can impress a teenager.

Once he turned his focus onto me. I was a shy person and a reluctant talker, and being the focus of attention always made me nervous, even when something I said drew a smile from the girl I had a crush on. So I squirmed when Langa asked me if I had a girlfriend. No, I lied, even though my friend Jomo and I were seeing two girls from the same home.

Did I know the neighbour's girl? Wasn't she about my age? Yes. Probably.

It was left unsaid that I was expected to prove myself soon.

My father worked at the taxi rank in town, and auntie would tell me each evening about her conversations with him, and pass on any messages for me. Each morning I would give her my replies, telling him I was well, and sending greetings to my mother, brother and sister. Then she would leave in her saloon taxi, the preferred size of car for township taxis because they took only five commuters, whereas my father's van took twelve to fifteen and wouldn't leave until it was full, which annoyed short-distance commuters.

One Thursday after auntie had left for work, I decided I would go and see my father.

Auntie's township, Peddie Extension, was a tightly packed cluster of multi-coloured bungalows on the side of a low hill west of the town. I set off down the same gently sloping road that the workers followed each morning, passing the field where learner drivers were taught, then the police station, to reach Main Street. It was midday when I reached the taxi rank, and with the taxi business being rather slow on a Thursday, I found my father easily.

It was an unseasonably hot winter, hence our need to stay in the shade, and I wanted to ask my father for money to buy myself some sandals. I found him – a quiet, peaceful man of forty-six – standing with two colleagues beside one of the taxi vans in his usual "uniform", a golf-shirt and faded blue jeans, without a jersey or jacket.

I was a reticent child, even with my own father. Later in life, when I had shed some of this trait, I realised that although I could be open with other people – old people, lovers, relative's children – the male children of my age were generally as formal with their own fathers as I was with mine. This is how it must have been for our fathers with their own fathers. Xhosa society in their generation was rigidly segmented into age groups, and all were required to keep to their designated places. Particularly in the cattle kraal, the arena of Xhosa manhood, the gospel according to age dictated who ate and drank what and who did what – newcomers did the brunt of the work while the old men directed operations. In this environment, being even slightly emotionally available to one's son opened a father to charges of mollycoddling, to be frowned on by his peers as doing the boy no good.

My father was in any case not given to conversation, and so that noonday in July we kept the exchange short and the greeting and goodbye brisk.

How was the family doing back home in the village? I enquired. Good, he said, everyone was well. How was I getting along at auntie's house? I was enjoying myself, I answered truthfully.

I asked him for the money and he enquired what it was for. When I told him, he handed me a R20 note.

My last words to my father that day as I left were, "I'll be going now."

Did neither of us have any more to say, or did I fear the little Asian-run shops would close, perhaps for their Muslim owners to say their midday prayers? Or did I want to get back to auntie's to finish a task? I don't recall. I don't even remember going to see auntie at her fried fish and fruit stall in front of the local Spar supermarket in the town centre.

"Okay," he said.

The next day was Friday, and the weather was pleasant when I woke up. As usual, I had a wash, ate breakfast and did some jobs around the house. In the early afternoon, when the younger children of my cousins returned from playing in a nearby field, I hung around with them outside in the shade, reading old copies of the *Daily Sun* while the radio played in the house.

In the early evening I sat with Monde on the front stoep, admiring the glimmering streetlights of Peddie and the beams of the cars tracing the line of the N2 highway that sliced the town in half. To the east lay the civic centre, to the west the business district – the Nozukile Spar, Pep, Jumbo, Just On, FNB, the Post Office, two funeral parlours and a trendy night club called Satisfaction. All the traffic was travelling either from King William's Town in the north towards Grahamstown in the south, or vice versa.

At about six that night, auntie arrived home. I remember the scene clearly.

The children spotted auntie's taxi as it finally showed up, but instead of driving up to our doorstep as usual, the taxi stopped abruptly a short distance away. Auntie staggered out of the back door with her hands on her chest as if out of breath. There was a little commotion as the other passengers all got out after her, four strangers looking as surprised as we were.

Monde, the children and I all stood up, craning this way and that to see better. Our voices must have alerted those inside the house, because they too came out to look.

Now all the doors of the taxi were wide open, and my auntie was being escorted by people on either side of her, her arms wrapped around their necks as she walked, like an injured rugby player being led off the field by medics. They advanced so slowly that I thought of going to help, but then decided I should keep to my place, which I did.

I was at the gate as auntie reached the house, and I followed behind as she and her helpers entered the house.

Monde and I busied ourselves carrying auntie's wares into the house. Then I went to sit in the "lounge" area, trying to listen while she quietly sobbed in her bedroom compartment, with relatives crowding around her trying to comfort her.

There were no raised voices from the adults or the children; there was no Lionel Richie, no radio playing, only quiet voices and muted sobs.

It was as if something had happened that was too tragic to speak about.

When nine o'clock came, I went to bed.

I was still a child in the deepest sense of the word, and I had yet to experience pain.

Two

UNCLE VUYANI ARRIVED EARLY in the morning. It was Saturday, and although auntie only took Sundays off, she did not go to work as usual. I thought it was to be expected that uncle Vuyani came to enquire about his eldest sister's wellbeing. Auntie had a history of heart problems, and I had concluded during the night that this must have caused the incident the previous evening. Uncle spent some time in the house before meeting me in our cramped kitchen, his voice unusually low, unlike most weekends when a few glasses of beer made him jolly.

"You have to go home to Prudhoe," he told me in a casual tone.

"What's happening?" I asked, barely curious.

"A traditional ceremony is taking place there today."

Having been raised in the Christian church, I felt no interest in my Xhosa culture. But it didn't occur to me to question why I had to be present at the ceremony, even though the holidays weren't even over. I merely asked why I hadn't heard about it earlier, and whether he would also be coming. This may sound sufficiently inquisitive, but because of my shyness, my enquiry was voiced with great respect.

My uncle told me he would attend, but neither he nor anyone else was to go today, except for my grandmother Magatyeni. I must accompany her, he said, as she was old and might get lost. And she was already waiting for me.

Reluctantly I agreed, seeing this as only a momentary but necessary favour. Grandmother was the one leaving, not me. I would take her to the village and then return as soon as it was permissible, to finish my vacation.

The last thing I did was go outside to hang a pair of jeans on the clothesline. I didn't even return to say a goodbye to those in the house, who were all very quiet and unlike themselves. Only later did I understand that they were too shocked to pretend otherwise.

Grandmother and I set out for town on foot. Only once on our way did she ask me to stop so she could rest on the side of the road.

"We should buy tea and sugar in town," she said. When I agreed, and suggested the closest Pakistani general dealer I knew, she repeated, "We cannot go home without tea. You can never go home without tea when there is a ceremony."

When we got walking again – it wasn't a long road, but *makhulu* Magatyeni was already in her seventies – her sluggish stroll dictated our pace. But this was fine with me; I was in no hurry to get home. I was wholly uninterested in the journey, and had none of the sparkle of glee at returning home after a holiday. When we finally reached the taxi rank I felt our pace had been too brisk.

We were just about to take our seats in the taxi van – grandmother already had her hands on the canopy door and one leg poised on the upturned beer crate – when uncle Vuyani materialised. He motioned us to a corner of the rank with gestures that I now recognise as edgy, and spoke to grandmother in a low voice, as if embarrassed.

Suddenly I noticed my father's taxi – the old Mazda Drifter van that had seen better days – parked in front of a hawker's caravan in a corner of the rank.

Strangely, there was no one inside. It looked abandoned.

"Where's my father?" I asked uncle Vuyani.

"At home," he answered.

"Then how come his taxi's here?"

It had an engine problem, he told me. A mechanic would take a look at it.

Now other relatives appeared at the taxi rank. My cousin Thulane* from Prudhoe had driven them all to town in the Toyota Corolla of a distant relative, who was with him now, along with my auntie Bulelwa, cousin Sakhele and *bawomkhulu* Mncedi, who was technically my uncle, but so

---

* Not his real name

much older that we referred to him as "eldest father", the equivalent of grandfather.

With no desire to leave Peddie, I was delighted to see these relatives. Now grandmother Magatyeni couldn't get lost, I reasoned, so I could return to auntie's house and avoid the ceremony.

No, no, said uncle Vuyani firmly. We will all go together.

To this day it still surprises me how swiftly and easily I acquiesced. How normal everything seemed to me then. It is all the more impressive when I consider in full the trip that followed, all of us going home to a traditional ceremony as if there was nothing amiss. How good uncle Vuyani was, thinking on his feet and improvising answers to counter my growing suspicions.

Years later I tried to recall whether there were any signals that I missed that could have indicated to me that this was a ruse. Some word out of place, some change in the mood, some look in the eye or a rueful grin as a result of trying too hard not to show vulnerability or sadness at the taxi rank that morning among all those relatives who already knew the truth. Surely there was something – anything! – that said: *Ndoda*, something's up.

To this day, I come up empty.

The village of Prudhoe where I lived lay to the southeast of Peddie, less than an hour's drive away, the last of a cluster of villages called eMazizini.

There was little traffic as we headed south on the N2. The Corolla was in front with all the relatives I had met at the taxi rank, except for Sakhele, who was in my group. We followed closely behind in my dad's taxi – the engine seemed to be working just fine. Occasionally passing taxis would honk and flash their lights as they recognised my father's taxi, and we honked back.

We kept to the slow lane, talking and looking around at the scenery through the windows of the canopy. At first I marvelled at the town of Peddie that I had yet to get to know well. Then I admired the Nompumelelo Hospital on a low hill just as we left Peddie, and later I watched the villages come and go along the road, with names I always mixed up. As we got further away there were no more villages for a while, only farm fields now and again, squares of brown earth in the faded green turf. The sight didn't exactly make me homesick; but it made me reminisce, at least, about returning home after previous school holidays elsewhere, or after shopping trips to town with my mother and siblings when she had bought us new clothes and I couldn't wait to get home and try them on.

Soon we turned left and entered a hilly region of thorn veld, where rolling hills stretched as far as the horizon. The tarred road grew rougher with every gear change, and potholes and vegetation began to encroach on its margins as it meandered through the hills. I felt as though I was floating when the car dipped down, before accelerating up the next hill. At the top might be a village or at least a cluster of brown brick houses, a mud rondavel with a kraal enclosed by bush and a vegetable patch, grass fields replete with cattle, a soccer field or even a cemetery with crosses and headstones sinking into the ground.

This was the journey that my father made every single day with the joy of a man who had seen far worse times.

I didn't feel the remotest interest in the conversations that took place in the car, and barely remember any of it, though I must have participated. There would have been the usual comments about our surroundings among the old members of my family. The environment was always important to the old folks, particularly the lack of rain for sustained periods, in ways that I didn't yet fully grasp, and they would comment just as city tourists do when venturing into the countryside. Cousin Sakhele no doubt remarked that he hadn't seen this part of the Ciskei for a long time, and uncle Vuyani would have noticed how it had changed, and how it was clearly short of rain, just like his area.

There was no end to the villages. My father's taxi was easy to identify because he always marked the brand names on his tyres with white chalk, so that at high speed the tyres appeared to have a white stripe. Recognising it, commuters on the roadside naturally tried to flag us down, but we didn't stop.

As soon as we passed a village we speeded up. Potholes took over the road as we snaked endlessly through the hills – up and down and up again – until we came to another village and slowed down again.

At the village of Mphekweni we entered a gravel road. This slowed us down considerably, and we drove for what seemed like forever, rushing around the curves with dust bellowing on our tail. We passed the village of Mgababa, topped a short rise, and then levelled out again before a settlement came into view perched on a bed of low rolling hills. Prudhoe.

The village was dotted over flat hills, sliced into three pieces by a dying stream. In front of the houses were kraals, and beside or behind them were their kitchen gardens. A place of little charm, Prudhoe was one of the few villages in the Peddie district whose occupants had been resettled there by the apartheid government, at a time when whites thought nothing of giving their own names to settlements of uneducated blacks. Once a thriving agricultural area, by the late 1980s the farming community had dwindled to just a few pineapple farmers, and thatched huts and tin-roofed bungalows began to sprout in place of mealies and wheat. I had learned this from my elders during many conversations in the cooking compound, where we sometime sat long into the night roasting mealies during harvesting season.

We took the first turning and continued until we reached the bottom of the hill west of the village. Despite my reluctance to leave auntie's house in Peddie, my feelings changed as soon as I saw home. Returning after a holiday always filled me with a mixture of regret and joy, and so it was this time.

Our house was a decent size, four rooms in all, built of concrete blocks with a tin roof. My parents, my two siblings and I lived in an extended family of twelve that included older cousins, an uncle and aunt, and *makhulu* Nodabadini, my father's mother and the family matriarch – a headstrong woman with a tight *doek* and a passion for tea.

The house was roomy enough for all of us, although my three eldest male cousins slept in separate mud flats in the yard. But it was not a wealthy household. When it rained heavily we had to stuff old clothes under the kitchen door and position drinking pails across the floor to catch leaks from the roof, which had no ceiling. The blue paint on the outside walls was always faded, as though suggesting, rightly, that my parents ought to spruce up the house more often than only at Christmastime, when a fresh lick of paint made the village houses look more festive and appealing.

Our courtyard held a chicken enclosure with a generous brood and a kitchen garden in the back, where *makhulu* sowed maize, peas, pumpkins and other ingredients that went into the sort of mushy vegetable-dominated dishes she liked, and probably reminded her of her old life on a farm. There was an outdoor toilet and a cooking compound that was really a shack with gaping holes for windows. Dogs were only kept by those who enjoyed hunting game in the nearby KaQhola and KwaJoji forests, so when we obtained a puppy it was not as a companion, and caring for it was not a favourite chore. When the sad puppy died after a few months, no tears were shed. But cats were a different story. We always had one or two because my mother loathed mice and the damage they inflicted on the food bin at night. As children we got excited when our cat and dog would growl and snarl at each other, and enjoyed watching them have a go at each other.

It was already afternoon by the time we entered the yard and stopped in front of the house.

All the right elements were there: volumes of clothing on the clothesline signalled house-cleaning activity, old village men were seated on chairs by the kraal, and women were milling about the yard with pails of water and wood-fire pots.

My sister and younger brother came out to greet me. I was grinning broadly, suddenly aware that I had missed them terribly, and they smiled quietly back. I entered the kitchen, enthusiastically shaking hands with each of the village mothers I found there, all busy making tea, washing dishes and kneading dough for baking.

I was still greeting relatives in the kitchen when cousin Thulane interrupted me and led me into the master bedroom, with the band of relatives and elders I had encountered at the taxi rank trailing behind me. After entering the room I sat on a bed and the others stood facing me in a semicircle.

I was still smiling and looking around at the faces encircling me, confused by all the fuss and wondering what it meant.

"Thabo," Thulane said. I turned around to look at him enquiringly.

"Your father is no longer with us."

The shattering cruelty of those words came with that instantaneous flash when you realise you have been deceived. "A traditional ceremony," uncle Vuyani had said. But *makhulu* Magatyeni had brought tea and sugar in place of the obligatory bottle of brandy; no one had ululated to welcome our arrival at the ceremony; my mother had not appeared; stricken eyes and quiet smiles had greeted me as I shook hands.

Tears welled in my eyes.

"He is dead."

I began to sob.

Three

LIFE AFTER MY FATHER'S DEATH began the moment I finally located my mother in the lounge and collapsed in her arms. "Oh *mntan'am!*" she cried as both of us sobbed. She was sitting on a grass mat surrounded by the women closest to her: my grief-stricken grandmothers Nodabadini and Magatyeni, one of my mother's sisters, other more distant female relatives, close friends and the village grandmothers. Such is the tradition during the grieving process among the amaXhosa after the passing of one's husband. According to custom, a brief prayer followed.

After a while I got up and left for my parents' bedroom, where I stayed until early evening, not only because children weren't allowed to be with their grieving mothers during those first few days, but also because I had nothing else to do.

I retreated into myself in the days that followed. When I looked at the faces of those who came to offer condolences, I believed that no one had ever suffered as we were. This was my general mood after our tragedy. I went about feeling numb. I couldn't begin to say how exactly I felt about the calamity that had befallen us all. I simply walked around in a daze.

Day 2, Sunday: The first thing I had to get used to was the presence of all these other people, both inside and outside the house. Grief in our culture was community property. People from my parents' Gospel Church of Power arrived in the afternoon to hold prayers and a church service. For the next two weeks, we were to be inundated by groups of visitors from various churches where my father was known, as well as from related clans, workplaces and former organisations with which my parents were connected.

Day 3, Monday: This was the first working day after my father had died. Uncle/*bawomkhulu* Mncedi and auntie Bulelwa travelled to King William's Town to identify my father's body and get it transferred to the morgue in Peddie. They also brought home his belongings: his wallet, identity papers and some of his clothes.

Day 4, Tuesday: Life at home was nothing but a blur. My father's body was now at the morgue in Peddie.

Day 5, Wednesday: More and more villagers descended on the house, and house-cleaning began. The old men in coats and woolly hats congregated at the cattle kraal, where they built a fire and talked and smoked until they felt they had paid their respects to the departed. Mourners came to relay their condolences and offer prayers; and village mothers took over the cooking compound to provide food and drink for the family and all their mourners.

Day 6, Thursday: Every relative and family friend had by now been alerted, and the funeral date was set for Saturday, 19 July, fourteen days after my father had died, to allow enough time to prepare everything.

Day 7, Friday: Colleagues from my mother's workplace visited the house for a short prayer. The prayer routine was established by now: mourners arrived and prayers were held in the late afternoon. My siblings and I had only seen our mother throughout the week when we needed something she alone could help us with. For the rest she was kept secluded by the other women.

Day 8, Saturday: More relatives arrived. My holiday at auntie's house in town was now long forgotten.

Day 9, Sunday: A church service began in the late morning and continued until the early afternoon. There were people all over the courtyard. I was beginning to get used to the situation.

Day 10, Monday: The funeral was a communal activity, and preparations began to pick up speed. The late afternoon prayers were now attracting growing numbers of people from the village, the view being that if you didn't show up at the funeral of others, no one would turn up at yours.

Day 11, Tuesday: People started repainting the house and sprucing up the courtyard. The rooms were all being prepared for the impending visitors.

Day 12, Wednesday: Work continued around the house and yard. Kinsfolk from parts of the Eastern Cape arrived. A neighbour escorted my mother and us three kids – Thabisa, Sino and me – to King William's Town. There we bought new clothes for the funeral. On the way back we stopped at the mortuary in Peddie. From the outside the building looked like a general store, with tombstones and name plates leaning against the wall with price tags attached. A man wearing an overall and rubber gloves led us to a cold, dark room, speaking to us calmly all the while. On what looked like a hospital bed, he lifted the cloth covering my father's face, and showed us where the bullet had entered his head. I was numb to everything, and I just stared.

"As you can see," he said, pointing. "This is where the bullet went in. It came out this side."

I could barely comprehend what he was saying. The bullet … this side … that side …

Afterwards, as we walked back to the car, my mother said, "It was his time. When God decides, you can't do anything about it. You just have to accept it."

Day 13, Thursday: The young men from the village went in a hired tractor to collect wood for the fires that would burn for the next two days.

Day 14, Friday: This was the last day before the funeral. The old men of the village, who were overseeing the daily activities, started setting up the big tent. The young men, meanwhile, congregated at the local cemetery from early in the morning to take turns digging the grave. When they returned in the afternoon, a bull was slaughtered, and an all-night vigil began, which continued into the morning of the next day. Throughout the night there was singing, preaching and clapping followed by more singing, preaching and clapping. Still more relatives arrived, and were welcomed with a prayer to thank the Lord for their safe trip. There was more singing, more preaching and more clapping. The whole procedure felt like a dream, but at some point I crept away and fell sleep.

Day 15, Saturday: The funeral day. The morning was sunny. The first order of business was carrying the meat from the bull to the women's cooking compound. But this was not my job. I spent the early hours serving my elders, helping them to get breakfast and make their preparations for the funeral. I ironed for whoever needed ironing and fetched hot water for whoever needed to bath. When they were all ready, it was the turn of us youngsters. Just as I began my own ablutions, I was told that I could see my father's body one last time, but I chose not to. My private viewing at the funeral parlour had been enough.

Cars began to line the road outside as the whole village arrived, including all my father's colleagues from the taxi rank. Prayers began in the big tent in the courtyard, the mourners' plaintive hymns filled the air.

The funeral began shortly after ten o'clock. The wind came up as cousin Thulane read out my father's obituary, and then various other adults – some who had known my father as a child, and others from his work or the church – each got fifteen minutes or more to speak about him. They all said kind things, how nice he was, how bright, how dedicated, how humble.

All this time my mother sat on a grass mat beside his coffin at the centre of the tent, surrounded by the same women who had stayed at her side ever since my father died. My sister and I sat out in the sun in total silence at the edge of the tent, just as we knew our father would have wanted us to. This was the kind of behaviour he encouraged when we attended church services.

For me, the ordeal was surreal. I felt no connection to the process or the events taking place around me, which continued from the early morning until about five in the evening.

One of the speakers was Mzwandile Gwejela, a taxi colleague of my father, who outlined the circumstances of his death. The Peddie Taxi Association to which my father belonged, he explained, had a simmering rivalry going with a taxi association based in King William's Town. Recently these two organisations had been forced to operate from the same taxi rank in the King William's Town CBD, and now their animosity had spiralled into full-blown warfare.

In the days leading up to my father's murder, each association had been sending its members to carry out overnight stakeouts at the amalgamated rank to safeguard the primacy of their association's space. On that fateful day after I saw my father, he had travelled to King William's Town, where he was among a small group of owners staying over in a minibus to guard their position in the central rank.

In the early morning, my father's group was startled by the noise of rocks battering their vehicle. They were under attack. In a blind panic, they leapt out of the taxi and made a dash for it, every man fearing for his own life. A single gunshot rang out as they ran. Later, when things had calmed down, the police called to tell them that someone had been killed. It was Gwejela who had gone to identify the body.

Four

My father was a taxi driver. He was murdered.

Long after the funeral, I went on obsessively replaying this picture in my mind – my father being shot in a stakeout gone wrong. And yet to me his death remained unreal.

I knew about taxi violence. I had heard of drive-by shootings leaving a victim's car pockmarked with bullet holes, of execution-style killings in remote spots on the edge of a city, of balaclava-clad assassins gunning down a taxi driver at his front door and fleeing in a waiting car. In my youthful ignorance, such stories had never engendered anything more in me than an immature satisfaction over a juicy piece of gossip.

But hearing of my own father's death left me in stunned

disbelief. It was so unlike what I understood the usual taxi violence to be. Yet I clung to this picture of his death, and each repetition brought on flashes of powerful emotion – agony, anger, self-pity.

As time wore on I began to adjust certain facts to protect myself. I gradually condensed the whole account by omitting the painful parts, padding out the comforting aspects, and making the whole scenario shorter and blunter until it was drained of emotion. Only the skeletal details remained – the gun pointing at my father, the killer pulling the trigger, my father collapsing.

I didn't realise then the risks of reducing my father's memory to a single agonising moment. This was never my plan. I didn't wish to pretend that I had been with him on the last day of his life. Nor did I have any masochistic bent to "see the moment" and go through the pain of his death again and again in an effort to understand it better. I only took comfort in knowing that my father must have suffered little pain before life escaped from his body. He would have died before he realised what had happened.

On my first day back at school, I picked up right where I left off, in the naïve pretence that my life would continue as if nothing had changed. Although the pain of loneliness clung to me like a physical presence, I had no difficulty concentrating. I suffered no anxiety or panic attacks. But I was convinced that no other person could ever understand my pain.

Not once did any of my fellow classmates give any sign that they knew what had happened. They knew of course. How could they not? They didn't avoid me, however – far from it. But they were sensitive to my situation, and no one asked questions. One way or another, I now realise, everyone I knew must have caught wind of my father's death, either from the radio or the newspapers. And word of mouth would have taken care of the rest. Yet for the next two and a half years until I matriculated at the age of seventeen, not a word was said by anyone at school about it.

Nor did I ever mention it to them. Not to the teachers, not to the schoolchildren, not even to my friend Jomo, who had arrived a little drunk on the night of the vigil and tried to help with chopping up the slaughtered bull for the funeral. The only comment I got from a classmate after the holidays was that my complexion had darkened. I explained this by recounting my holiday in Peddie.

But I was growing dark on the inside too. As everyone must also have known.

How could I possibly talk about his death? The only way I had ever heard people do so was through levity, by making jokes and laughing about the quirky antics of the deceased. I could not contemplate broaching the subject of my personal tragedy in that way. It seemed too insensitive to my departed father, too embarrassingly personal, too cloying, too debasing.

This reticence made it even harder for me to endure those rare conversations in which my adult relatives – only the women, never the men from whom I took my cue – spoke about my father without sounding too sad, although I sensed that they were.

"You're like your father in so many ways," sighed auntie Bulelwa, the younger of my father's two sisters, after not seeing me for a while. Was her remark perhaps inspired by the five o'clock shadow covering my face – my boyish attempt at being a man – or that slightly stooped walk of my father like an old woman foraging, my downcast gaze partly reflecting my bashfulness?

"You're just missing your baby brother," I said lightly.

"Yes," she agreed, as if that settled the matter.

My continual mulling over the moment of my father's murder continued. Trying always to visualise it meant that I focused on the agonising part of his story – the killer's finger, the gunshot, his falling – rather than on accepting his passing.

By my final year of high school, I was a loner. This wasn't so much because I was avoiding people, but because I was studying a lot. I withdrew from socialising entirely, except for study group sessions with a couple of classmates. In the end I achieved the only university-entrance pass in my year at our poor village school, which had no library or computer lab, only broken windows and a collapsed ceiling. Only twenty per cent of our class of 2005 passed at all.

My high marks pumped up my ego and gave me some status in my village. But this didn't help me deal with my emotions. I suspect that my family were overawed by my academic accomplishment. I gave the impression that I knew it all and didn't need help from anyone. I was proud and independent, and wanted to do everything myself.

What I didn't yet know was that the less humble you are, the less willing people are to offer help and advice, because you are less likely to listen.

Five

IN JANUARY 2006, I went to live with auntie Bulelwa in the city of Port Elizabeth, or eBhayi, a couple of hours' drive south of Peddie. I had visited briefly in the past, when auntie was nursing in Kirkwood just outside the city. But now I was here to study at the Nelson Mandela Metropolitan University, and I was about to be "schooled" in more ways than one – books, music, politics, independence, experience …

All possibilities seemed open, and I had the idea that I could pick from a wide range of personas. I had my own ideas about who I was, and I felt I was a whole lot more than just a taxi owner's son. After all, I had matriculated with the highest marks in my school.

To my enchanted eye, studying journalism would be a walk in the park. But I failed to anticipate how enormous and terrible the cultural shock would be. Suddenly I was buffeted by all that was foreign to me. There were wonders, undoubtedly – chocolate brownies; monkeys on the campus lawn; music that touched me deeply; people my age announcing with confidence, "Me? I disagree with you, ma'am." I was mingling with whites, listening to strange ideas like the need to wear sunscreen, and hearing my peers speak the Queen's English, which left me too mortified at first to mumble back in my own broken speech.

I was soon painfully conscious of how little I knew about the world. I had a mountain to climb and no safety rope.

Looking back, I can only laugh at Thabo Jijana the village boy, entirely devoid of personality with an atrocious sense of fashion, a squirmy voice and a deficiency of opinions. I was a lost sheep without a Jesus to find me. I was so wet behind the ears that I took forever to realise that I was entering a life for which I was never intended.

I can only guess what my bemused classmates must have thought. *He should show more interest in girls. Too stiff! This poseur needs a drink! Prepare for a serious deviation, boy. You're in the city now!*

In such an alien environment, I soon began to sense my own exclusion. And yet I also gained a clearer understanding of who I was. I had been so assured of my place in the village back in Peddie that I had never before questioned my sense of belonging. I had passed matric well and thought myself gifted, but in a room full of high achievers I wasn't even in the game. Living outside of my familiar context, it was like being an exile, an immigrant. Day by day I discovered how little I had in common with my classmates, which made it so much harder to fit in.

Finally in my third year, after flunking only one or two subjects, my struggle to cope began to show. All of a sudden, life wasn't much fun anymore.

Journalism had been my second choice after I found the intake for marketing already filled. My enthusiasm for the profession had stemmed from reading old copies of the *Sunday Times* brought home by my mother to scrub windows or wrap china. I enjoyed my studies for the first couple of years, until I realised it would require me to work among people, sniffing the air, ears pricked to identify newsy controversy. But as a person who didn't like to talk, I couldn't see this as my chosen profession.

During my fourth and fifth year I began to flounder. I couldn't seem to pull myself together. I disengaged from the university's social life and retreated into myself more and more. I was skipping classes, writing poor essays and earning poor grades. I started spending too much time in the library, finding solace in reading. But even when I was completely immersed in such delights as the stories of Barbara Kimenye, I was never truly happy. Finally in 2009 I dropped out of university.

During those last years at university I began to really miss my father. The smallest things kept prompting memories of him. I was pained by things as commonplace as a father and son walking together down the road, a TV show being touted as "family time", or being told that someone's father would be fetching him after class. All were brutal reminders of what I had lost – the guidance of a father, the warmth of a complete family.

I began smoking cigarettes and drinking alcohol, but they turned out to be very temporary remedies. I started chasing girls, without any regard for their class, personality or morals. Yet I always felt alone.

These were all distractions, efforts at forgetfulness.

I barely allowed any outward sign of distress to show, except for keeping to myself at auntie Bulelwa's house, withdrawing completely from class discussions and neglecting whatever girl I was seeing. And I caved in to my long-held doubts about God.

It felt like I was locked in solitary confinement. I sat alone, fighting my demons. I had not shed a tear since that moment in my mother's arms when I learnt of my father's death. I no longer knew how to cry, although I cried inside. The emotions I had done my best not to release through words or actions were finally, after a long and agonising delay, finding expression in other ways. I was clearly depressed.

My delayed mourning process had begun.[2]

On the bus home after class one afternoon in 2008, I was absorbed in James Baldwin's *Notes of a Native Son* when a line in his book struck me like a hammer blow: "I had not known my father very well."

Reflecting on the death of his father, Baldwin's words could have been mine. He was black, he grew up in a Christian church, and his book was published when he was twenty-seven. He acknowledged the moment of his father's passing as a pivotal point that changed his life. "When he was dead," Baldwin wrote, "I realised that I had hardly ever spoken to him. When he had been dead a long time, I began to wish I had."

Something softened in me. Baldwin was opening a door, showing me that a man could speak frankly about his innermost feelings. By now more than five years had passed since my father's death, and in all that time I had carefully wrapped my grief and loss beneath a blanket of smiles. I had never expressed anything to another human soul about the loss of my father.

"My father was a taxi driver. He was murdered."

These were probably the most difficult nine words ever to roll off my tongue. It happened during a news-writing class in one of my senior years. We were each required to name a traumatic event that had significantly affected our lives. We divided up into pairs, as if for a priestly confession, but without any of the privacy or allure of a Catholic booth. I was paired with a girl from Kimberley who had been at boarding school, and she described how she'd been cornered in the hostel bathroom by a girl who wanted to find out whether she was gay or straight. Then I told her about my father's murder.

Just those two brief lines: "My father was a taxi driver. He was murdered."

Afterwards I felt good about having done this. Talking about it had felt natural, more so because this other young stranger had opened up so easily to me. It was as if I had finally been given permission to talk about his death. But I still found it difficult to confront his murder without condemning the injustice of it, and so my telling ended with the shooting, referred to in the vaguest terms and without dwelling on it.

But at least I was finally able to speak of my father's murder to another person. I was no longer avoiding telling the truth. And bit by bit, it became easier. When a lecturer doing research for her master's thesis interviewed me about my background later that year, I told her too. A few months later, during email correspondence with a writer I admired, I let slip that I intended at some point to write about my father's death. Like Baldwin, I realised, writing could be a way to triumph over my depression, by forcing myself to confront the truth and deal with the pain of losing my father.

Later, in a student hangout in Grahamstown after a few drinks late one night, a girl made an unprompted disclosure about having being raped. In turn I revealed that my father had been killed in taxi violence. When she then asked about my father, I realised how little I knew about him.

Who was he? What was his story? Now that I was finally able to speak about my father, I developed a newfound interest in him, almost a craving, to discover more about this man whose blood still ran through my veins.

Six

STRANGELY, THE FULL FORCE OF MY PAIN at losing my father only hit me now, although his death was already a distant memory. My family was growing accustomed to his absence, and talking less and less about him. But I hadn't forgotten him. When I returned to the village during the holidays, his absence always made him intensely present for me, as if he had just walked out of the room, leaving his scent behind.

But it had alarmed me to notice, after one December spring-cleaning, that all the things that reminded me of him – his clothes, his gospel music cassettes, his yellow metallic bowl – were gone, or had acquired a new character through reuse.

Photographs became his last remaining presence in my

life. Paging through our family album, I would stare at each picture of him for a long time. In many he kept a straight face as if posing for a mug shot. This was all I had left of the man who was still so much a part of me, yet had been snatched away before I had any real sense of who he was. There he was again, but freeze-framed, lifeless, confined to a piece of paper. What were the stories behind all these photographs? How much more was there that I knew nothing about?

Unknowingly at first, I began to seek out information about my father. Whenever I was with my relatives, I did my best to get them to tell me stories about him. I would sit with auntie Bulelwa or with uncles or cousins, urging them to tell me more and more. I even wanted to know about his father, his father's father and how various other people were related to us.

Afterwards I returned to the photographs of my father with a fresher eye. I wanted to understand him. And secretly I kept hoping to recognise something of myself in his look and his manner.

And so, with the help of my relatives, I gradually began to piece together the stories of my family and get a broader picture of my father's life and background.

My ancestors, it seemed, could not have been left untouched by the cattle-killing frenzy of 1856–57, when a young girl named Nongqawuse led pockets of amaXhosa to destroy their crops and slaughter their livestock. She had prophesied that spirits would reward them by sweeping the foreign settlers into the sea and delivering a more prosperous life. The 1820s had brought a wave of British settlers into this region, and as the Xhosa nations lost land to both British and Dutch settlers – who had their own ideas about who owned what – their region became a spider's web of borders and warmongering chiefs. Fort Peddie – named after a British commander – had been founded by the British military in 1847 to protect amaMfengu refugees evicted from Gcalekaland, where black nations had been at war.

When the promised events of Nongqawuse's prophecy failed to occur in 1857, widespread famine soon decimated the population. The amaXhosa, one of the few southern African tribes to have fought the British colonists, now became a nation living from hand to mouth at the mercy of their conquerors. In one fell swoop a nation of pastoralists became farm workers, their men "boys" and their women "servant girls".

By the time my father's father *bawomkhulu* Magala was born in Gcalekaland, sometime between 1905 and 1910, the settlers had firmly established their power over my people.

Bawomkhulu Magala was a farm worker from a young age. Like my father, his Ciskei *dompas* tells me he was born in eDikeni, or Alice, where he worked for a British settler family. Alice was just a village then, and hadn't yet shed its settler roots for a more commercial style of farming. After my grandfather's first wife died in childbirth, leaving him with two children, he took a second wife, my grandmother Nodabadini Seyimani. She was younger than him by at least fourteen years.

Uncle/*bawomkhulu* Mncedi, the family historian, says only that we are amaXhosa, but because of the 1990s SABC drama, *Ityala Lamawele*, which was based on a true story, I suspect my ancestors were of the Gcaleka subgroup. The twins who fight over their father's estate in this TV series carry the same clan name as ours, Nzotho, and the drama is set in Gcalekaland at a time when the settlers had started calling this area home. The amaXhosa in the drama retain their traditional institutions and culture, with messengers of their traditional court travelling long distances by horse to debate cases; several characters also refer to the Age of Enlightenment, indicating that Christian missionaries had arrived. According to uncle/*bawomkhulu* Mncedi's concise history of my lineage, *bawomkhulu* Magala's father was Jijana, and Magala was his firstborn. Mncedi was the eldest child of *bawomkhulu* Magala's first marriage. The five children of Magala's second wife, Nodabadini, my biological grandmother, included Bulelwa, NoKrisimesi and my father Fundisile.

My grandfather and his brother were so close that wherever one brother went, the other was sure to follow. When Magala went to ask the bride price of my grandmother, he brought along his younger brother Mpukwana, who fell in love with her younger sister Magatyeni. So the two brothers married sisters.

Grandfather Magala's employer, Vernon Cummings, owned two farms, one in Alice and the other in Peddie, another settler town much like Alice, with a good source of water and swathes of agricultural land. The Peddie estate lay among a sprawl of others in the fertile eMazizini area, which had productive farmland, cooler weather, low hills, sparse forests, and fresh water from the Great Fish River.

White farmers had been drawn to this area because its earlier denizens had depended on farming for their livelihood, producing pineapples, maize, dairy and wheat.

It was an annual routine for the farmer to move with his employees and their families between both farms, spending half a year at each one. This nomadic lifestyle took advantage of the seasons and the different climates and conditions on the two farms to make more money. The Alice farm lay in a heavily forested region, which protected the livestock from the cold in winter. In summer, however, it got stiflingly hot, so the farmer moved to Peddie to stave off the risk of death to his livestock. While in Peddie he grew pineapples, whereas in Alice he grew mainly mealies and wheat. July to December was thus spent in Peddie, and January to June in Alice.

The trip from one farm to the other was always an event in itself. While the farmer's family and their belongings travelled in horse-drawn carriages, my grandparents, along with the other five labourers and their families, followed with the livestock on foot, like a party of refugees fleeing war. Although it is barely an hour's drive from one town to the other, the journey on foot entailed a gruelling week's hike across the wilderness, following beaten footpaths around towering mountains, along steep seasonal riverbeds and up and down gravel slopes. I have traversed a similar route myself to visit relatives in that area, where little has changed – the roads are still gravel, road signs scarce, and villages scattered between dense forests and fields of wild grass.

My grandparents had to build their own mud houses on both estates. When they left for the other farm, they would leave a distant relative or a young man to watch over their property until their return.

My grandmother had her first child, my uncle Xhantilomzi*, in the early 1940s, although his passbook wrongly recorded it as the 1950s. My father, the seventh and last, was born in Alice on 3 December 1957. Being too young to manage the journey, my father was left behind with relatives in eDikeni during the annual relocation to Peddie. The whole family – my grandparents and their older children – had to leave without him, so that my father was raised only intermittently by his parents during his earliest years, until he was old enough to move with them to Peddie.

In the mid-1960s, when my father was about eight, the farmer settled permanently in Peddie, and they made their last expedition from Alice. The farmstead in Peddie was named kwaKerry by an earlier farmer (presumably called Kerry) who had left before Cummings took over. *Bawomkhulu* spent much of his day working in the yard of the farmer's large colonial homestead, earning £2 (the equivalent of R2 then) a month. My grandfather's house was a mud-and-wattle rondavel and a one-roomed flat within walking distance of his employer's home. He also kept his own dogs and a few cattle and goats.

Food was in short supply for his family of nine, and carefully rationed. The family received a 24-kilogram sack of maize each month from the farmer, which *makhulu* Nodabadini ground with a millstone and then cooked into *umphokoqo* or *mieliepap*. Each morning *bawomkhulu* returned from

---

* Not his real name

the white man's kraal with a pail of fresh milk, most of which went into the elders' tea rather than to the children. *Bawomkhulu*'s small pension paid for other foodstuffs such as sugar, tea, yeast and soap that ran out long before pension day, which only came around every second month. Many years later, auntie Bulelwa still recalled going out as a young girl clutching an empty bowl, to ask a neighbour for some mealie meal because they had none left.

When my great uncle Mpukwana arrived late for work one Monday after a Sunday of drinking, he was fired, and he and his family had to move nearer to the town. This was why his daughter, auntie Nolwandle, now lived in a township in Peddie.

The lives of the farm workers were tough. Happy moments were rare, according to auntie Bulelwa. Other than in traditional ceremonies, beef was available only when one of the cattle that ploughed the pineapple fields died, and the farmer allowed his farmhands to help themselves. When word spread of a binge of red meat, the messenger usually arrived with bloodied hands as evidence, and they would rush to where the beast had collapsed, to find the men already hacking off chunks on a first-come, first-served basis. Such unplanned events, as unremarkable as they sounded to me, broke up the humdrum of their lives and provided brief moments of drama and delight.

Because *bawomkhulu* Magala worked at the main house, he was exposed to what a better life looked like. The whites lived in splendid isolation from their staff, with absolute authority over their means of survival – cattle herds, land and wages.

They raised their own chickens, toughened creatures that lived on mealies and whatever else they picked up in the yard, the sort today called *inkuku yesiXhosa*, which are considerably tougher and need longer cooking, but are delicious, requiring little flavouring beyond a pinch of salt. Pigs were fattened throughout the year to be slaughtered at Christmas, a time when there was little work and lots of carousing.

Gradually new foods began to appear at the local store. Polony was viewed with suspicion by the elders for being "pink as a dog's tongue", and my cousins called rice "worms that don't move". You could buy a handful of cheap sweets for twenty cents, although the general store was an hour away by foot over the hills, and twenty cents was a rare thing. Children in those days did not demand money as their right.

Boys and girls went bare-chested then, wearing only an *inkciyo*, a little patch of cowhide tied around the waist to hide the genitals, although castoff adult's shoes were popular treasures. The T-shirts, jerseys, underwear and socks my generation took for granted were so rare that they were considered abominations.

My father may have been poor, but his childhood was free and happy. The boys spent all their time in the veld looking after their family's livestock, hunting mice and birds, eating wild fruit off the trees and swimming in dams. Such was my father's childhood in kwaKerry.

Around 1965 he started school, which meant he now had to wear pants and a khaki shirt. By then his older sister Bulelwa was already at school, despite the disapproval of her parents, who considered it a costly investment unlikely to yield a pleasing *lobola* when a girl's true career was marriage, domesticity and childrearing. Such was the norm for women then. But auntie had had her own ideas and no one was going to stop her from getting an education. About fifty children attended Tatshana Lower Primary housed in two simple stone buildings near kwaKerry. It was an Anglican missionary school that taught children up to Grade 5 in four classrooms. The Anglican Church was already well established in the area by the time Peddie had become an agricultural town, but by the 1960s only a few white people remained.

"Your father was the only child our parents had to persuade to go to school," *da'bawo* Bulelwa tells me. "He always wanted to be independent, but he was something of a loafer."

One morning, she relates with relish, she was ready for school before my father was even out of bed, so she left for school without him, never expecting him to bother to come on his own. Their busy mother had no spare time to chivvy him along the dusty 15-minute route through farmlands and forest. But during lunch break, auntie Bulelwa discovered him at school, looking as unkempt as if he'd spent the night in the woods. It turned out that their mother in a fit of rage had roused my father with a stick, and when he still wouldn't go to school, she had chased him with it all the way to school.

This was the only time *makhulu* ever set foot in the corridors of education. But my father never missed another day of school.

After four years he progressed to the Junior Primary Mpheko, two villages away in Mphekweni. Despite his indolence, my father enjoyed school, and got a first-class pass in Form I (Grade 8). But by then he was itching for something better than the humiliating poverty of his childhood. He was now smoking and drinking, and he never returned to start senior high school. He was going to Port Elizabeth, he announced, and off he went.

By then several family members had already joined the steady urban migration from the rural hinterlands. Uncle/*bawomkhulu* Mncedi, the first to set off for the city, was now living in Port Elizabeth. His brother Xhantilomzi had gone off to the mines of Johannesburg. Auntie NoKrisimesi and auntie Bulelwa had also joined uncle/*bawomkhulu* Mncedi in Port Elizabeth – NoKrisimesi was a domestic worker and Bulelwa was nursing.

By the time my father left for Port Elizabeth, the apartheid government had declared the Bantustans or "black homelands" based on ethnicity, and the Ciskei was born, a slice of the southern Eastern Cape that included Peddie. Young people were practically fleeing their parents' villages for the urban life.

One night in 1971 my father appeared on the doorstep of uncle/*bawomkhulu* Mncedi's shack in one of Port Elizabeth's oldest townships. The household included his wife and his son, Sakhele, and other relatives besides Bulelwa and NoKrisimesi. Every couple of years the entire household ended up relocating to some other part of Port Elizabeth, sometimes because they were forced to move by the apartheid policy that limited the growth of black settlements, and at other times to improve their chance of getting a government house. So from KwaZakhele they moved to Veeplaas, then to Mgababa, and later to Zwide.

During my father's primary school years a teacher had given him the English name Richard, and in the city he now took his mother's surname, Seyimani, to become Fundisile Richard Seyimani. By then blacks were adept at flouting rules to get work permits, and uncle/*bawomkhulu* Mncedi, whose papers also used the surname Seyimani, posed as my father's legal guardian.

At that time, says uncle/*bawomkhulu* Mncedi, he watched my father transform into a man. He took his driver's licence to escape the murderous drudgery of unskilled labour, and secured what were considered to be good jobs – he first worked as an electrical apprentice with the municipality, and later as a bus driver. It seems he had found a sense of purpose in life.

In 1978 auntie NoKrisimesi died of TB. Soon afterwards my father was robbed on the way home from work late one evening. Although only his belt was taken and he wasn't really hurt, my father was so incensed that he vowed to do something about it. A few weeks later he enrolled for karate lessons at the local sports club. Eventually my father took his revenge on the local bully who had robbed him. In fact, the story goes, the culprit was so impressed that, sometime later, he even asked my father to teach him some karate moves.

But violence continued to stalk my father. The 1980s was the most violent decade in the history of apartheid, and bus boycotts often ended with a necklacing. My father was by then driving a municipal bus, which put him in grave danger.

One day his empty bus came under attack from township residents, and my father was lucky to escape with his life. He decided it was time to quit.

With his savings and his severance pay he bought his very first taxi, a second-hand Toyota HiAce. And with it he began operating his own minibus taxi in the townships.

But my father had a weakness for the pleasures of the Friendly City. He began drinking heavily and sought comfort and entertainment with the wrong crowd. He became a ladies' man, and fathered two children out of wedlock. The girlfriend he took up with was a bad apple, and he even visited *sangomas* with her. This signalled to auntie Bulelwa and the family that he was clearly troubled and looking for help in the wrong places. He might as well have been bewitched, because he was rapidly descending into a life of carousing and alcoholism.

It was auntie Bulelwa who called him aside for a talk about the direction his life was taking. "Mother wants you back at the farmstead," she told him. "And I think you should go."

So in 1983, my father returned to Peddie, where he secured a contract with the Fish River Sun Resort to ferry staff. Yet, far from reforming, he continued to drink, and still attracted women like moths to a candle. Several times he was arrested by the authorities over offences such as drunken driving, resisting arrest or assaulting an officer.

Then he met my mother and made her his wife.

Seven

My parents knew each other from the Real Tigers Sports Club, the only one in the village. My mother, Nokhaya, was a member of the girl's netball team, while my father played for the men's rugby side. One afternoon, when my mother went to visit a married girlfriend of hers, my father was also there visiting, as a relative of her friend's husband. Talk of *lobola* and marriage began the very next day. Soon afterwards, in 1987, my parents married.

In many ways my parents were opposites. My mother was slender with a light complexion, while my father was tall and dark skinned; she was friendly and warm, while he was even-tempered but quiet; she was a teetotaller who went early to bed, while he stayed out drinking till late; she held to traditional Xhosa customs, while he did not; she was a high-school graduate, while he had dropped out after Form I (Grade 8). Both their fathers were farm labourers, but my mother was the eldest daughter and second of six children, whereas my father was the youngest son and the last child of seven.

I was born in 1988 in the district of Peddie, along with my twin sister, Thabisa. My mother was twenty-one when Thabisa and I were born, while my father was already thirty-three. My grandfather *bawomkhulu* Magala had died the previous year, so I never met him.

Any Eastern Cape child who has passed through a crèche probably knows the nursery rhyme[3] based on our names:

Intaka ezimbini zikhwele emthini,
Amagama azo nguThabo noThabisa,
Bhabha Thabo buya Thabisa,
Bhabha Thabisa buya Thabo.

Although our birth was normal, I was kept at Nompumelelo Hospital for a few weeks after my sister and mother were allowed home. I like to delude myself that I was the cutest and funniest newborn at the infants' ward, from whom the nurses couldn't bear to be parted. But in truth I probably had jaundice, because my eyes, my mother says, were as yellow as the insides of a fattened rooster, and had to be shaded from the light as I lay in the neonatal intensive care unit.

My family was then living at kwaKerry where my father had grown up. But when the "homeland" or Bantustan of

Ciskei was created, the white farmers had left en masse, unwilling to live under a black administration. As a result, the farmsteads in the area had degenerated into little more than dry fields with derelict stone cottages where none of the farm workers wanted to live anymore.

At first we clung to our old life and our little mud house, while neighbour after neighbour left to make a fresh start in a new community. But in 1989, two years after my paternal grandfather died, we relocated to a nearby settlement made up of families just like ours – Prudhoe.

I remember nothing of our life in kwaKerry, and so I think of Prudhoe as the village where I was born and raised. I have always called it home.

Apparently I was a curious child in both meanings of the word – I was inquisitive and adventurous, as well as sometimes an object of interest myself. Unlike me, my sister was always the one to play safe, even before we outgrew our nappies.

My mother was the breadwinner at that stage, and had to return to work as soon possible. So for the first years of my life, my auntie Bulelwa, a stay-at-home mother with her own adolescent boy, often babysat us.

If I didn't get my way, she says, I would cry a river. Once, when she bundled me onto her back and took me to town, something got into my stew, which was nothing unusual.

"I couldn't figure out why you were crying so loud," she tells me, her laugh-lines crinkling. "So I tried giving you a pear to stop you crying. But you gobbled it so hurriedly that strangers in the street were convinced you would choke." So she gave me her prize ballpoint pen instead, which I promptly hurled down a drain in a rage. I only quietened down when exhaustion finally overcame me and I slept.

Prudhoe is not far from the Indian Ocean coastline, often referred to as the Sunshine Coast. On clear days when we were out rambling, fruit-picking, swimming or herding, I would stand on an anthill and gaze at the sea, a blue haze that stretched all the way to the horizon. That was where you went to "make money" in my parents' time.

My father still had his Toyota HiAce minibus when I was born, with his contract to transport staff to and from the Fish River Sun Resort, a half-hour drive from our village. My mother was a waitress at the Mpekweni Sun Resort, not far along the coast from the Fish River Sun, and under the same ownership.

My father's lifestyle was no different from that of many a young father of his era. There was plenty of drinking and women, along with all the quarrels of a young marriage, in which the squandering of money figured a lot, and caused my mother a great deal of grief.

Sometimes my mother just couldn't stand it. On several occasions in my early years she went back to her father's home, taking my sister and me, until she and my father resolved their issues and she returned to him. This was not considered unusual in their generation. It was felt that any young marriage had to go through some pain and drama until it found a stable footing. Each time my parents had a fallout and separated, my father would come to visit us at the home of my mother's parents, which is remarkable, as visitation rights were not the norm then.

"He would fetch you and your sister," my mother tells me, "and take you for a drive in his kombi around the village, or to town or somewhere else." She knew this only because we would tell her where we had been when we returned. Who knows if this was part of my father's plan to win her forgiveness. My sister and I were too young to remember these trips, but we always enjoyed outings with our father when we were older.

It is a testament to my mother's affection for us and her yearning for a better life that she had photos taken of my sister and me by the village photographer. These required booking him for a house call, much like the doctors of old times, and paying a deposit when he took the photo. The remainder was paid when he returned with the developed "cards". These photos now document the early years of our lives.

In one, we are two infants lying on the bed in matching outfits. In another, we are toddlers standing by the wall of the cooking compound as the sun sinks behind tall oaks in the distance. Thabisa is looking at something beyond the frame, while I stare straight at the camera, hands clasped in front of me.

There is one photo of my mother seated on a bed, cradling me on her lap as if to quieten me after crying. The background walls are bare and the bed clearly old, but the coffee table is laden with objects – deodorant, body lotion, shoe polish, a toothbrush, an ashtray, a bar of soap and a pack of cigarettes. I have my hand to the side of my head, as if it hurts or I don't want to listen to anything my mother has to say. My mother stares coolly at the camera. But with such deep sadness in her eyes.

Eight

WE WERE BACK TOGETHER all living with my father again in 1991 when I woke up one morning to find the HiAce gone.

It is a trial for my mother to talk to me about the times that pained her the most, especially the periods when my father was out of work and there was constant worry about money. She mumbles about my father's behaviour at work growing errant, about him drinking and being unreliable. It seems that his irresponsible lifestyle had frittered away the money he earned, and finally he was forced to sell the van. So poor had we become that it was unaffordable to maintain.

Around the age of four or five I remember once hearing the roar of an engine at daybreak, and an aunt or my mother called out, "That's them." Outside I found my father circling the house in an old maroon saloon car with my three cousins and a friend inside.

Did he have a temporary job of some sort, or was he helping someone he knew? I don't know and no one else remembers. But the HiAce was already gone by then.

However, the proceeds of the sale of the HiAce, combined with money saved by auntie Bulelwa, who was by now nursing in Port Elizabeth, was enough to build a brick house for our family. Since arriving from kwaKerry, we had been living in shacks and a mud flat. Now at last our household of eleven would have a decent roof over our heads.

This house was no small achievement. I confess that not long after I began primary school, I indulged in a lot of cheap, arrogant talk about My Home. It was a source of enormous pride and joy to me in a village where many houses were built of mud and wattle. In the school playground I was always quick to point out to a new classmate our sky-blue bungalow on the hillside. "I live in that house there," I would stress. "You see that one? That is our home."

There were other children who lived in houses just like mine, give or take a few minor features. But there were poorer families too. My innocence made me blind to the pain of their poverty, but from early on I knew that even driving a taxi had made my father someone to be envied, because he had work. And work meant status.

In addition to my parents, Thabisa and me, our household included my father's elder brother uncle Xhantilomzi, his wife auntie Nomzamo,* my father's mother *makhulu* Nodabadini and my four cousins. Two of these cousins were the children of my uncle and auntie, one was auntie Bulelwa's son, and the other was the child of my father's deceased sister.

Uncle and auntie had been working on a pineapple farm near the Fish River Resort, run by the last of the white farmers. They were clearly paid peanuts, or they wouldn't have pilfered the fruits of their labour to sell around the village or to share with us. But around the same time that my father lost his job, the pineapple business closed and they both lost their jobs. Uncle took to doing minor jobs around the village, but he also began frequent spells of hard drinking.

My four cousins were all still at school, and *makhulu*'s pension couldn't fill an empty foodbin, no matter how crafty my mother and auntie were when month-end was a long time coming. It was a struggle to stretch whatever we had until God sent us manna from heaven, so it fell to my mother to take responsibility for our household.

I was too young to understand the distress of my family's finances, so it failed to dampen my spirits or cloud my childhood memories. Romanticised as they probably are, my memories are all happy ones. I remember riding a metal drum with my best friend Sihle as if it were a horse, rocking it sideways until I fell and broke my arm. Once the pain wore off, I had great fun scaring my sister with my plaster cast, pretending it was an AK-47.

I remember vividly not minding the rain on Christmas

---

* Not her real name

Day in 1991 as we dressed up in our new clothes early in the morning – dungarees were in fashion then, and Thabisa and I each had received a pair. We spent most of the day going door to door asking for sweets, treats or even money, like trick-or-treaters on Halloween. This kept us busy and no doubt gave our parents a pleasant break to relax and enjoy themselves. The tradition had emerged among my parents' generation, when farm children were too poor to afford the Christmas luxuries my generation now took for granted – new clothes, festive food and a whole day of play. Their generation remained amazed at all we took for granted, and never failed to remind us of how much harder things had been when they were our age. According to *bhut'* Fezile, jam on bread was strictly a Christmas luxury. My mother says she never owned more than one pair of shoes – her school shoes – which were always bought too big to make them last. Uncle Xhantilomzi insisted that children rarely got meat, except at Christmas when a goat or chicken was slaughtered. At a traditional ceremony they would crowd around their fathers with outstretched palms in the hope of receiving a scrap of the meat they were eating, even just a bone.

The disdain with which Prudhoe's youth now view this dying ritual is greatly mourned by the old folks who have stuck it out on the farms, even after the going got harder, corroborating their suspicions that the new South Africa after liberation is not the biblical New Jerusalem with streets of gold and healing waters flowing. The irony in post-apartheid South Africa, where more black people have become middle class and being working class is not as bad as it once was, is that poverty is now viewed as a choice rather than a misfortune – and a shameful choice at that.

It is hard to imagine how my mother alone managed to put us through primary school without us ever going short of clothing or school supplies. Not that we had everything we wanted – we were certainly not the Khumalos every village kid tried to keep up with – but we were never forced to wear hand-me-downs or go to school in takkies or socks full of holes, as some village children had to. I also realise now how much easier it is to study when you are comfortable. When you aren't it can be hellish.

But in my father's case, this time of hardship brought about personal transformation, or at least the desire to change. Unemployment had drained the joy out of his life, and with no money to go carousing or attract loose women to his arms, my father must have realised it would be foolish to risk divorce.

Separation was not unheard of for married couples at that time, although it was severely frowned upon for a wife to return to her father's home. A good wife was expected to stick out the ups and downs of early marriage, and it brought disgrace if she broke this unspoken rule, especially if she had already borne her husband's children. Returning to her father's house also made it easier for a disappointed husband to demand the return of his *lobola*. No doubt this ensured that many women put up with physical abuse.

However, my mother was the main source of income now, and perhaps this was the inspiration my father needed. In 1992, he stopped his drinking and became a member of the Gospel Church of Power. This church was part of the rising trend of African independent churches in South Africa, which subscribed to a strain of Pentecostalism and African spirituality. There were branches from Port Elizabeth to Cape Town, tailored mostly to Xhosa-speakers, with much talk of out-of-body experiences, the end days approaching, the repentance of sins or the wrath of God – the usual coercions.

On 9 August 1992, my father was baptised during a one-off church trip to Nyanga township in Cape Town where the Gospel Church of Power had its headquarters.

"I waited to see," my mother tells me, "if he would stick to his word."

It was a significant decision in my father's life. Almost overnight he exchanged smoking and alcohol for a bible and a suit. My mother was soon won over by his newfound salvation, and in no time they were both frequent churchgoers. This was when my father became the man I remember so fondly: a lotto-playing, boxing-watching, middle-aged man with an afro carefully combed and patted each morning like a manicured lawn, but with a beard perennially in need of a shave so that he looked a bit like John Matshikiza.

And it was through a fellow churchgoer that my father received an offer of employment in 1993. There was an opening for a delivery van driver at a grocery store in Peddie. He would need to commute to town from our village each day, and do deliveries between King William's Town, Peddie and the surrounding villages. He accepted the job.

I was five in 1993, and to give us a head start in life, my parents thought it best to enrol us in a pre-school run from the home of a teacher at the edge of the village. I enjoyed spending time with other kids, and it gave my sister and me a solid educational foundation, instilling in me an appreciation of learning that I have never lost.

All the boys my age had one favourite type of toy: cars. We made our beloved objects by hand out of wire. They were easy-to-make disposable sculptures. Mine, of course, were always vans like my father's. When I was very young, my cousins made them for me, until I learnt to construct them myself. Once I became proficient I began helping others with theirs. I remember these creations fondly. They were fast and nippy, almost like the real beasts. All we needed was a hammer and enough wire of various thicknesses – the thickest wire for the steering wheel and thinnest for binding our works of art together. I even tried to make an articulated truck once, but it was like an advanced class in architectural design – with the extra-long carriage, additional wheels, elongated steering wheel and complicated driving required, it was just too elaborate to pull off.

I chose our cooking compound as my assembly plant, and there were endless upsets whenever the women of the house, "my many mothers" as I called them, accidentally stepped on one of my masterpieces in the making.

TV also fascinated me in those days, fuelling my wild imagination, and cartoon shows like *Pokémon* stoked my interest in the creative arts.

Nine

ONE DAY IN MARCH 1994, my mother disappeared. When my sister tried to find out where she was, we were told she had gone to the hospital.

"To do what?" I asked.

"To buy a child," we were told. "A brother. Your brother."

And so Sinovuyo became the twelfth member of our family. His name was soon shortened to Sino.

This was also the year my sister and I began primary school. Because our house was built on a hillside, leaving for school demanded a determined uphill trudge, whereas returning home was a mere lazy downhill gallop. Although I loved my sleep and at first resented waking up in the dark and marching up the steep hill, my annoyance soon melted away. Nothing can even remotely compare to the joy I felt during this phase of my life.

Tatshana Primary comprised two crowded brick buildings beside the road leading out of Prudhoe. Our motto, borrowed from the Old Testament, was *sontinga ngokwamakhozi* – "we will soar like eagles". Our middle-aged principal, hardly the embodiment of a soaring eagle, looked like she had stepped out of a Can Themba short story about married women devoted to society balls. From the start we were thrown into endless school functions where everybody cheered us deaf, even though the sports events were far too disorderly to give any real pleasure (unlike our games outside the school gates), and our school choir only once made it through the first round of the local competitions. At the age of six, my sister and I marched up and down the aisle in a school beauty pageant, and won a prize as the adorable twins. Later, at a fundraising bazaar for a tour by the choir to which I belonged, I gave the welcome address to a roomful of teachers, parents and schoolchildren. After reading out a speech written by my teacher in English, I was praised for my reading – my first piece of literary encouragement. I positively glowed.

The only shadow over this period of my life was on the home front. In 1995, my father again lost his job. After two previous accidents with his employer's car, the third was the last straw for his boss.

My father began to spend his days at home doing very little. He was a discreet person, and tended to retreat to his domain, the bedroom, where he reclined on the bed, reading or writing.

Presumably because of his earlier experience as an electrical apprentice, my father now dedicated some of his idleness to studying the basics of electrical wiring and how to fix electrical appliances.

He threw himself into this new work. Within months, word had spread and he began to receive calls to do jobs in other villages. These odd jobs didn't pay much, although he had no complaints.

But our existence remained precarious, as few villagers called for an electrician, and even when they did, my father came cheap, so he kept on looking for higher-paying work.

This spell of hardship, just as when he first joined the church, seemed to increase my parents' determination to look to God. The Bible reassured them that hardship was something Christians should expect, even demand, as a test of character.

If my parents were frequent churchgoers before, they now became devout. Although no one else in our household or our extended family converted, there were a few other fellow churchgoers in the village, and all week long we would join these families in prayer meetings at a member's house, a routine that Thabisa and I quickly tired of. The big service was on Sundays in eNyeleni, seven villages away. We would all dress in our Sunday best – my mother in a long skirt and matching jacket, my father in his grey suit, Thabisa in her summer dress, me in decent pants and a shirt, and Sino in his baby clothes.

But whatever strength my father found in the church, he knew he couldn't continue long without better-paying and secure employment. Uncle Xhantilomzi had by now begun his descent into alcoholism, which would later claim him.

Then, in the summer of 1998, my father was offered a steady job – driving a taxi van based at the local rank in Peddie. He accepted. My father's new co-workers at the taxi rank soon recognised his piety, and took to calling him by the biblical nickname Mzalwane.

Although my father's new occupation wasn't well paid, it had its compensations. The owner of the taxi, who had been born in Peddie, was now based in Johannesburg, sometimes on the mines and sometimes driving buses, so my father was barely supervised. He reported to the owner's wife, eight villages from Prudhoe, and only had to stop at her home after his last trip each afternoon, where he counted out the day's takings with her. The car "slept" at our house, and my father was at liberty to set his own working hours. He enjoyed the freedom this gave him. And without any of the restrictions and imposed order of employment by an official institution, my father was able to earn additional income by accommodating side contracts to transport municipal employees, or take church groups on special trips.

It was a turn for the better for our family. Even as children we recognised this, probably more so because we never ran out of ideas as to what to ask for when we knew month-end was approaching.

Our prayers, as my mother liked to say, had been answered.

The taxi van was a second-hand 1991 Mazda Drifter. It was white, the colour of choice for South African taxis, and bulky as taxi vans tended to be. My father treated the car as his own, and took good care of it. A few years later, when the miner bought another taxi van, my father bought the Mazda from him and became self-employed, something I suspect he took great pride in. He never worked for anyone else again.

To us children, the taxi was there for the sole purpose of taking us on weekend outings. He would often take us to town with him after church on Sunday, where he refuelled it for the start of the new week. We never tired of our attempts to ensure that it was used towards this end, and as soon as the weekend began we set to work. Sino had to do the talking while Thabisa and I prodded. This was our way of avoiding being accused of disrespecting our father by speaking to him too directly. At four years old my brother was considered too young, and no word out of his little mouth could amount to an insult. So he became our appointed mouthpiece.

"When are you taking us to town?" Sino would ask as our father sat down with us to watch the news on TV, or joined us in the kitchen while our mother cooked supper.

"Soon," my father would answer.

He had a low voice, which he only raised on the few occasions when we had given him reason to, and then we knew what would follow – a belt, a sore behind and a life lesson.

"You have been promising."

"I know."

"Where will you take us?"

"I'll tell you then."

"Is it to town?"

"Wait till Thabo has washed the van. Then we will talk."

I can still glimpse my father at the rickety kitchen table,

and hear the clink of his spoon as he eats his chicken and rice. As I approach the taxi with a pail of soapy water, I can see its tyre tracks still pressed into the grass.

Some nights my father worked late, and we would wait up for him, watching *Generations* on TV with our mother while trying to finish our homework or any house chores we had been given. As soon as the car lights flashed past the kitchen window, I would watch the door, waiting for him to walk in and say hello. He was always tired and reeking faintly of engine fumes, his sleeves rolled up to the elbow and his hands often caked with oil. My mother would take the plastic shopping bag he was clutching and hand out any scrumptious snacks my father had brought home. If she was out waitressing at the hotel on night shift, Thabisa, who many assumed was the eldest child, would take her role as we sat around the TV, dividing out the treats so that we all got equal shares.

Friends during those years were made not so much at school but in the village playground, on bird-hunting excursions or while swimming in the dam. Each year I seemed to have a new best friend, until another displaced him the following year. People were always relocating, and several of the children I knew then I have not seen since. And as I passed to higher grades I lost contact with any friends who did not progress.

My only constant friend was Thabisa, my twin sister and partner in crime. Anyone who knew our family agreed that she had my mother's beauty, while I never felt I took as strongly after my father. There were moments when Thabisa and I didn't get along – we were forever fighting, as kids do – yet we were close, as twins so often are. To a degree this was because we spent so much time alone together while our parents were away at work, so Thabisa and I often played together or helped each other with our chores. When our mother worked the day shift, she left home at four in the morning before we woke up, and returned around seven in the evening. When she worked the night shift, she left in the afternoon just as we arrived home from school, and returned at six the next morning while we were getting ready for school. But once or twice a week she had a day off.

Like any typical village boy I loved soccer, and I took every opportunity to wander in the nearby woods, swim in dams or pick fruit. Thabisa envied me going out so much while she stayed home, and I envied her for being the responsible one that our superiors always addressed.

Both my sister and I were very happy at school, but we also liked going on holidays, perhaps me more than her. Once in those early years we wanted to visit auntie Bulelwa in Port Elizabeth, and hatched a plan to get our father to take us. As the gutsy one, it was me who had to ask. My sister and I spent a whole day scheming about which words to use to persuade our father, firing questions at each other as if preparing for a job interview.

"And if he asks why we want to go?"

"Tell him auntie asked for us."

"What if he says we should have asked sooner?"

"Tell him we didn't know we wanted to go then. But now we do."

Finally I approached my father while he was resting in his

bedroom, and asked if he would drive us to Port Elizabeth.

"Why not take a taxi by yourselves?" he responded.

I stood in silence, looking at my feet. Because we're barely twelve, I wanted to say, because we don't have a clue which taxi to take, what to do when we get there, or even what Port Elizabeth looks like. Because we like going in your van and we want to go with you.

"At your age," he said, "I used to go to Port Elizabeth alone by bicycle."

I have never tried to confirm this claim with the rest of the family, but my father wasn't the kind to kid around. Port Elizabeth may be two hours from Peddie by car, but by bicycle it would have taken him an entire day, maybe more, of furious pedalling on a tedious road, exposed to the elements with nothing but a backpack and the clothes on his back, and nowhere to stay overnight for a break. Would he even have carried food if he couldn't afford to pay for a taxi or a lift rather than going by bicycle? I am reluctant to learn the answer. I find it uncomfortable to confront the poverty that made my father the man he was.

But in the end he agreed to take us.

Thanks to the Mazda, we always seemed to be going somewhere. Some mornings if my father was going past our school he would give us a lift; on weekends we often went with him to the Engen petrol station in town, to church, to fetch our mother from work, to aunt Nolwandle's Peddie township home, or even to the beach.

On my very last day at Tatshana Primary School in 2000, my maths teacher asked me to leave my exercise book behind to assist those coming after me the following year. It was the greatest compliment he could have given me.

Elated, I left for home with my school report tucked under my arm. As I passed Jama Senior Secondary School, I saw my father's van parked outside. It was payday, and he was waiting for any teachers who might want to go shopping into town. I went over and showed him my report. He studied it for a minute and then handed it back without comment.

"Keep it safe for your mother to see, too," was all he said.

"Yes *tata*."

Despite his silence, I sensed his quiet pride in us. Our parents always encouraged academic excellence. More than once I had overheard my father telling others how proud he was that he didn't need to force us to do our homework or help us through it.

I hurried on with joyful abandon to join my schoolmates rushing towards Prudhoe, eager to discard our washed-out school uniforms forever. The summer holidays lay ahead of us, before a new year and the start of senior secondary, a new school where we knew everything would be different.

Entering high school was a major transition in my life. I immediately developed an interest in girls, and began hanging out with friends late into the night. I was now a gangly boy and full of mischief. Although my school grades were always fine, I grew quite rebellious around the house. Thabisa and I had long since had an unofficial 5 pm curfew, but my sister tended to stay at home anyway, so it was really aimed at me. But this was the first unsaid rule I began to break. It wasn't long before I would be creeping into the kitchen after ten at night, assuming that my parents were sound asleep, only to be startled by my mother's voice.

"This is no time to come back home!"

Soon I moved out of home into a mud flat in the neighbouring yard. The property actually belonged to auntie Bulelwa who lived in Port Elizabeth. My older male cousins had each built themselves a mud flat in her yard before they finished school and left the village to find work, and I took over one of these when another family who had been living in it moved away.

One might expect that, as a taxi owner's son, I would have been impatient to get behind the wheel myself and learn to drive, but I wasn't. My father did once offer me a driving lesson, but it didn't go well. I wasn't yet fifteen then, and my moods were at the mercy of my hormones.

One Sunday morning Sino came to my flat and woke me with a knock at the door. Our father wanted to see me, he said. When I got to the main house, my father was walking to the car, and instructed me to get into the driver's seat and drive. That was his way. He didn't bother to sit me down and explain.

I wasn't an early-morning person, so even inside the car I tried to wriggle out of the exercise. "I'm tired," I told him. "Can't you just drive until we're out of the village?" He was annoyed, and it was a surprise that he didn't knock me senseless then and there. In the end, I turned the key and did as he told me.

Getting out of the yard and up the hill went well. Left foot on the clutch, right foot on the accelerator, and the brake in the middle. We reached an open field outside the village with no trouble. I was doing okay until he told me to stop and reverse. That's when it all went wrong. The poor shrubbery in that field has probably never recovered from that day. My father took the wheel and drove us home, and never tried to teach me again.

The high school itself was more extreme in many ways than primary school. Some of the teachers were doubly cruel, and loved to use the cane. But there were some doubly kind teachers too, who became almost like parents to me, and went the extra mile to provide support. It was a poorly kitted school with a low level of education, but thanks to the profound kindness of those individuals, when I headed off to university, I was filled with optimism.

Ten

WITH ALL THE BACKGROUND STORIES about my father finally filled in by my relatives, my own scant memories were now rounded out. At last I had a better sense of who my father really was and what he had meant to others. To his grandmother Nodabadini he had been Krwala – a nickname denoting a young man after his Xhosa initiation. To the government he was Fundisile Jijana or Fundisile Richard Seyimani. To his colleagues at the taxi rank he was Mzalwane, while to us children, secretly, he was Kariza, our own private reference to his legendary karate days before we were born.

And yet, the more I learnt about him, the more I realised how little I knew him. I had always believed that the dead deserved respect. Now I felt my father deserved more. He deserved understanding.

Yet I didn't know my father well. I regretted that. I ached for the lost opportunity of getting to know him better. I continuously reflected on the stories I had heard about him, staring again at the photos, trawling my own memories, trying to uncover the man beneath it all. I yearned to know him on a deeper level. Perhaps in all this lay a search for myself, for some deeper clue to my own identity.

We had caught occasional glimpses of his natural enthusiasm while he watched his beloved boxing on TV on Friday nights, goading the fighters like a true fan in his deep voice: "Jab, come on, jab! Don't give him space. Punch!" Yet despite his fighting background, not once had he translated this enthusiasm into a boxing tutorial or even just a discussion with my brother and me.

There is one photograph of my father in Peddie doing a karate kick, which a local villager is trying to block. This is the only photograph in which my father features with someone else. I was told that he was returning from the taxi rank when he stopped near home to chat to a neighbour. As the village photographer came up the road, they posed beside his taxi van for the camera. Was he nostalgic for his days in the city? What else did he remember fondly about Port Elizabeth?

His karate days in Port Elizabeth especially appealed to me. Before my father's conversion to Christianity, he had been a dynamic character I would love to have known. This was a man hardly recognisable alongside the one I knew as my father. During that earlier part of his life, it seems, he had been bursting with life and joy. What music had he loved when he was in the city? What political ideology did he follow? Did he ever grow indignant at the paradox of apartheid, where native Africans were treated like immigrant workers in their own country? How I wished I knew.

Whatever his life in Port Elizabeth had meant to him, he looked worn out by the time my sister and I entered this world. Perhaps his buccaneer life in the city had burnt him out. He had definitely had his fun, and now, having dedicated the rest of his days to God, he no longer sought the pleasures of life.

I don't remember my father having a lot of friends, except for a few fellow churchgoers who lived nearby. And yet, although he didn't talk to many people, people seemed to talk about him, judging by the stories I had heard – whether about the naughty things he did during his youth, or afterwards when he became the kind of responsible husband my mother deserved. He had indeed turned into a kind and steady husband. Yet he had never had a photograph taken with his own wife or children.

My father's face was always intensely serious, and he doled out warmth with caution, so that to us children he appeared unadventurous and far sterner than he really was. To this day, I cannot remember hearing him laugh naturally or seeing him carefree around my mother or other adults. Perhaps he was at times, but as a child I never witnessed it, so in my recollections of him during his later years he lacked the spark of life.

Maybe the poverty of his childhood in Peddie denied him what I now prize: the ability to put your own needs first, recognising that achieving your own happiness is the best way to have a positive impact on others. Perhaps poverty also starved him of the ability to express himself with ease. Whenever I had helped my father with chores, barely a handful of words passed between us. He behaved like someone who had been raised in a strict household, taught to speak only when spoken to, only when there was a real need.

Because of all this, I thought of my father as stern and aloof, although I see it differently now. Sometimes I catch myself in a moment of silence among a crowd of peers, and I recognise that I share more than a little of my father's character.

Although we too experienced some poverty in our own childhood, my father always strove to make us children happy, and he raised us with a paternal indulgence and higher hopes than he had received himself. I recall his gifts of toys for Sino, fancy hair products for Thabisa, my first bicycle at age twelve. Through these he instilled in us the awareness that we could still be happy even if we were poor. He showed his love not through words but through his actions, like the treats he regularly brought home for us after work.

The numerous outings my father took us on speak of the kind of available father he was, even if he did not express his love in words. One outing in particular has stayed in my mind. It was one of the few trips with him that did not go well.

Thabisa and I were about ten or eleven then, and we asked to accompany him to Port Alfred one Sunday evening, where he was going to refuel for the next day. Halfway there, just as we were going up a slight rise near the affluent seaside village of Kleinmonde, the van broke down. Our father told us to push the car down the road while he attempted to jump-start it.

I cannot recall the number of times we pushed the van that night. I kept expecting my father to give up, but he persevered. There was a routine to the business. We would push our hardest and the car would roll downhill, cough as if starting, and then die. Then we would run after the van and help him push it back up the hill, only to start over again. It was late at night, cold as hell and my sister and I were miserable beyond words, while our younger brother sat watching the drama from the comfort of the front seat. All the joy of the trip had long since evaporated, and we were sorely missing home, but we joked with each other to inject some pleasantness into our despair.

After an hour and much tinkering with the engine, my father at last gave up and closed the bonnet. He called his mechanic friend and was told help would only arrive the following morning. So he led us weary children on foot to the Kleinmonde police station, where we slept on the wooden benches in the main waiting area until morning. It wasn't as horrid an experience as one might think. Rather than feeling fearful, I found it a great comfort just to come in from the cold, and I was deeply impressed by the commitment and resourcefulness my father had shown. To me, his determination to devise a plan at a moment's notice had irrevocably demonstrated that he was there for us in times of need, and always would be.

This was the first incident in my childhood that made me conscious of my father and the kind of man he was. After that I began to view him as a central presence in my life, rather than just another interchangeable character, as adults so often are to the children of extended families who share the love of many adults. I like to think that my childhood began to take a different direction from then on.

But he spoke so little that it was never possible to know what he was thinking. Having given up alcohol and his old lifestyle, he became rather a quiet man who was not outgoing by nature. Around the house he often chose to be alone. Whether in the bedroom or elsewhere, he would read his bible, study electrical circuitry or write in his diary.

It was with great joy that I discovered the diary he had kept during that time.

Although it is a 1993 diary with each page pre-dated, it appears from the opening pages that my father originally bought it simply to record the contact details of his acquaintances. Evidently it soon occurred to him to use it as a notebook to jot down his thoughts, which he continued to do for years, as some of his handwritten dates reveal.

My father's entries are varied and inspired. Far from chronicling what he had done each day, there were weeks during which he wrote nothing. What he wrote was never intended for publication, of course, and misspellings and grammatical errors abound. But for me it is a revealing document that offers insight into the mind of a man I hardly knew, let alone understood, and I found myself returning to it repeatedly as a window into his mind.

Much of my father's diary is written in capital letters, and mostly in English, reminiscent of the way he liked to pepper his speech with English words while delivering testimony at church. It made him sound "clever" among the largely uneducated congregation who worshipped exclusively in isiXhosa. But my father had a love of words and an ear for language, and apart from the Bible and *Bona* magazine, he usually read in English. His diary clearly indicates that he used his solitude, especially during his time of unemployment, as an opportunity to develop his thoughts and ideas. Several of his entries touched me deeply, for they speak of a man on the cusp of transformation, both personally and spiritually.

On the opening pages, where one might expect to find his name, address and other personal particulars, my father instead wrote:

God blessed me in 1995 in the name of Christ Jesus our Lord. Thank you Lord Amen.

There is no doubt that he found the bible interesting during this time, and it seems that he learnt a lot from it.

Sometimes he listed English phrases, many of which he might have discovered in biblical teachings.

Under 1 January, he wrote:

Perfect principles
Love Rejoice
Ignorant intelligence
Amazing grace
Disarm the enemy
Fellowship is a key note
You can't into 2 CAMPS
I was starving spiritually

> *It's a little difficult to speculate*
> *kusenzima ukutyabeka izityholo*

He also recorded with enthusiasm the moment he decided to teach himself the basics of electronics during his time of unemployment.

> *This date in 1996 God revealed his glorification by granting me the ever need I've been looking for in decades. So I thank u my dear Lord in the name of Lord Jesus Christ Amen. Issued money to despatch & receive the material of learning how to repair & service a T.V. & also video tape recorders & radio repairs.*

Another entry records:

> *I am an unskilled labour but also a mechanically minded person.*

Numerous entries are testimony to his religious devotion, from which he drew guidance and inspiration.

> *When trouble comes rejoice. God planned to clean up the mess by sending his begotten son our Lord Jesus Christ.*
> *God doesn't change, he is that same God that preserved 3 men from the fire.*

The following entry suggests the courage it took him to join the church when few villagers and no other relatives did.

> *People are so fearful that they fear even accepting God because they fear other people.*

His diary also reflects his philosophy of human relationships – the Christian benevolence that favours purity of the heart over outer appearance.

> *I don't bother myself about the quality of the skin. I only bother with the quality of the spirit.*

Another passage shows his conviction about the benefit of comradeship through the church.

> *We don't have lessons to learn but we have experience to share.*

At other times his entries were more philosophical.

> *There's trouble before success. U'v got to experience failure before you succeed.*
> *Never live in the past. Forget the past.*

He clearly applied this rejection of the past in his later life, as he never showed any inclination to revisit his history or share any of it with his children. What was it, I wondered, that he saw the need to forget?

Yet each time I closed his diary, I walked away unsatisfied.

Eleven

WE UNDERSTAND SO LITTLE of what is happening to us at any given moment. Only by remembering, by cross-examining the consequences, can we reflect on how we fared in times of tragedy and what the event really meant to us.

This is where a memoir can help us to salvage what we can from the doldrums of our past, and also, perhaps, give value where it is due.

When I first embarked on my quest to find out about my father, I told myself I was going to "interview" my past. At the same time, I began an interview with myself – an imaginary conversation. If the idea sounds absurd, I have to agree. That was precisely what I told myself whenever thoughts of writing about my father's death started nagging me. In my journalism-fuelled immaturity, I always considered memoir the pity party of illness survivors or the province of braggarts, whose success in life afforded them such an indulgence. I was the most unsympathetic reader of such books. But the more I read, the more I began to revise my opinion.

When I finally decided to write my own memoir, I had to face my own fears and self-doubts. As a strategy to overcome my fears, a fictitious confessional interview provided me the illusion of a sympathetic ear. Blame, if you like, the psychoanalysts who suggest we have multiple selves, or the poets who act as both author and subject. But only in the form of a "pretend interview" – a kind of interior monologue between myself and my internal critic – did I find the courage to say things I couldn't otherwise express.

While the memoirist in me tried not to quake like a nervous schoolboy outside the principal's office, my imaginary interviewer was an eager and hospitable confidante. I pictured us seated at a window table in a small-town café around midday on a weekend in springtime, when the air was fresh in the morning, warm at noon and chilly at night.

The interviewer opened the conversation.

Why do you want to write about your father's death?

To shed light on taxi violence in South Africa.

Is that your only reason?

Well, maybe not entirely. I also want to share a boy's meditation on how black men grieve.

Why do you want to write about this?

Because it took me over five years to even be able to

mention that I had lost my father, never mind to acknowledge my pain and allow myself to mourn. And even when I finally did, I still preferred to write about my feelings rather than open my mouth to another human being. I felt such a deep reluctance to share such personal information.

In five years, you never so much as mentioned your father's death? Not even to a friend, a relative, a girlfriend?

Never.

How is that possible?

That's what I'm trying to understand.

Experts describe the grieving process as a series of steps. Some divide it into three main stages: numbness, then disorganisation, and finally reorganisation.

In the first phase we are in shock and not ready to deal with our feelings. Nothing really touches us because we are numb to everything. We carry on as if we are on automatic pilot, going through the motions of life, attending to the funeral, the burial, financial settlements and our domestic life. We are living but not really reacting. This is when friends and family are needed to help us with chores and our daily routine.

Later, after the loss begins to sink in, we enter stage two, disorganisation. We have to start adapting to life without the help, companionship and support of the person we have lost. We may have the added burden of sorting out any unfinished business they left behind. Now our emotions start bubbling to the surface, like anger, shame, guilt, fear and sorrow. We miss our loved one, and reminders of them appear everywhere, constantly choking us up. We feel sorry for ourselves. We need to talk to others about our lost loved one, unburden our hearts and seek emotional support. It's very important to experience this anger and sorrow, and to allow ourselves to feel the pain of the loss. This is necessary for us to heal, but life at this time lacks the joy it once had, as if the sun has gone into hiding and refuses to come out.

This stage lets us progress towards reorganisation, when we start to rebuild our lives without that person, and find new outlets and interests. Friends and family can help by encouraging us to refocus our energy on the future.

Did you also go through this process?

Unfortunately not. It seems I got stuck in stage one. All those years I spent not talking about my loss meant that I merely repressed the emotions I felt. I was unquestionably saddened by my father's death. I felt sad for myself and for my mother, my siblings and the rest of our family. I missed my father badly. I was angry that he had been murdered, and I missed the life we'd had as a poor but close and happy family. But I never said a word about any of this to anyone, not even to my mother or Thabisa. I just lugged my heavy sack of unresolved grief around with me.

Were you given no reassurance that it was okay to feel upset about your father's death?

No. No one ever told me to give in to my sadness and allow myself to mourn. No one ever suggested that my bundle of grief would weigh me down. Perhaps no one in my life was any the wiser.

As a boy I had simply never learnt to cry when I felt like crying, to be sad and not hide it, to reveal rather than hide pain. I had never seen my father cry, nor any other man for that matter. A man was naturally tight-lipped, and could only show anger or retreat into silence when he felt deep sorrow. So that is what I imitated. This was what I understood was required of a man where I came from.

During my years at university, in addition to my struggle to adjust to city life and university, my pent-up emotional burden grew too heavy for my shoulders. But I didn't grasp that I needed to unpack it soon.

Was there no heart-to-heart talk with anyone at the time of your father's loss?

No. But of course, in a rural community, everything is shared. If you are successful in your career, you share your success with your fellow villagers, because the village "was always there for you". You might hold a little gathering and brew *umqombothi* or slaughter a goat to say thank you. It's the same with a tragedy – the community gets involved and helps with the funeral, for example, and if the family is poor, they help financially too. Grief is a communal burden in the village.

But finding peace after the loss of a loved one is up to the individual. There is no mandated emotional support that family and friends are expected to provide during grieving. And there is no real figure in my culture who serves the role of therapist or psychologist. Rather, there is a tendency to look to the supernatural whenever there is a personal calamity or an unexplained tragedy. Where unresolved grief affects villagers through strange dreams, perhaps, they talk of being bewitched, and this is viewed as the result of a transgression they have committed, or of a vindictive act by someone else. Then either a *sangoma* or a witchdoctor will consult the ancestors and advise how to make amends, usually through a traditional ceremony. In fact, some sort of traditional ceremony took place virtually every other month during my youth. That was why I so easily believed uncle Vuyani's story when he claimed I had to go back home.

Your mother was consoled by the women of the family when she lost your father. And how did the men grieve?

In my experience, talking directly about emotions was never an option. This can be hard for anyone, but for a village man there is a very real risk of making himself a laughing stock. This doesn't mean they are unthinking people. They are some of the most considerate people I have ever met. I think they often use traditional ceremonies and *sangomas* as an oblique way of confronting the deeper questions of life and death.

Do you think it has anything to do with education level?

I don't think education is a deciding factor. Despite what manhood meant to our ancestors, my grandfather's generation always said wise things to young men to help keep them on the right track. I don't think emotional expression from a man was as frowned upon among men in my grandfather's youth as it was among my generation.

Why do you think this has changed?

In my forefathers' time, I doubt that a close friendship between two men raised questions about a man's sexuality. Gay culture as we know it today is largely the brainchild of current Western enthusiasm. A man expressing his emotions was not as embarrassing then as during my youth. Men are now more self-conscious about how they conduct themselves in the eyes of the community, so they tend to cry inside only.

Are you saying it's only in your time that black boys have grown up keeping their emotions so tightly in check, just as their white peers fear being called gay?

Yes. I don't think it was as rare for previous generations of men to cry openly. I'm thinking largely of the men in my family and my village. If I asked the village men now what they would think if they saw a man cry in public, I would expect polite distaste. When I am back in the village I get the feeling that we are all supposed to be macho types.

Despite these rigid gender roles, do you ever find contradictions, like a young father single-handedly raising a child or a widow heading a household?

These aren't unheard of, especially in black townships. But they rarely change perceptions – a young man raising his child alone is viewed as an emergency, and a widow with five children is nothing to celebrate. The gender roles remain set in stone. But now I realise that women can teach men a few things.

Like what?

Like how to talk about their emotions, for one thing, and deal with emotional issues in less injurious ways. I know village boys who migrate each year to the city looking for better jobs and return years later in very bad shape. I know men so stubborn and proud to display any emotion that they become alcoholics, depressives and loners, strangers to their wives, children and community. I should know – I was heading down that road myself.

It must have been hard to write this book.

Before I made the choice to write about my father's death, it never occurred to me that because I didn't like to talk about myself, it would be so much harder than it needed to be. But even when I finally realised how tough it would be, I was determined to force myself through it.

What made you so committed?

I knew that writing was the only way I could come to terms with my tragedy. I knew I had to expose my feelings before I could finally close this chapter of my life and move on. This book, you might say, was my stage two. For so long I had kept quiet because I thought it was the manly thing to do. The real irony, when it came to tackling my depression, was that I had to be man enough to wage war on my deepest fears. The first step was to learn to be vulnerable. And that's where I finally began.

Also, having recognised that I wasn't unique in suppressing my grief, I hoped that by doing this I might set an example for others in a similar predicament.

In creating this outlet for your grief, did you learn anything? Did it change you in any way?

Yes, in many ways. I had to mature emotionally, and re-examine my identity as a young African man. I was forced to confront my inbred concept of masculinity. At moments when I grew fearful of facing the most painful parts of my life – such as having no one to turn to when my father passed away – a voice in my head would say: *Don't be pathetic Thabo, only women think like that!* I just couldn't express my feelings without confronting what it meant to be a man.

I suffered endless bouts of self-doubt, questioning my own

intentions, stressing about how my words might be taken by others, and battling my reluctance to lay bare more than the most basic facts of my history. I also had a dread of risking my father's name and reputation, causing him a second death by memoir, if you will. And then there was the ever-present fear that my narrative might be selective, revealing some things but still concealing others.

During the first few months of this project, I spent most of my writing time overwhelmed with dread, doing anything except what I found hardest – writing. I would scribble spiritual quotes, put on music, pin things on my wall ... anything to distract myself until I had used up the allotted time. Then I would go off and do something else, comforted by the knowledge that I had at least sat through the required period of torture. I trusted that eventually this process would get me to where I needed to be. In time I hoped I would move past my fears and be able to write more easily. So slowly but surely I soldiered on.

Do you think black men are more susceptible to this idea of a "real man"?

Being fearful of expressing emotions is not just a black man's issue. It is a burden shared among modern men. For every word like *isifebe* and *mnt'kamama*, white men have similar terms of derision – like sissy, mama's boy or wimp.

But my experience of it is through my own culture. Even before the age of reason, black African boys in pain, physical or otherwise, are told *"indoda ayikhali"*, a quasi-command passed on unwittingly from generation to generation. Because "real men" don't cry. This easily translates into "masculine" behaviour like heavy drinking, dominating women, and taking one's pleasures regardless of the harm it causes others. This attitude is all around us, and even reflected in advertising. Think of the woman's voice saying, "He's the real man because he uses Real Condoms", and the TV campaign in which actors, comedians, activists and boxers try to persuade men that a real man isn't determined by the number of women he has, but by how he protects his wife and cares for his family.

I think most of us absorb part of our concept of masculinity from our fathers. Inside my head a manly voice keeps saying: *Eh ndoda, the men reading this will say you're a soft one.* Our fathers in turn inherited the traditional ideals of the generation before them, which came from the generation before them, etcetera. This is not unique to African culture, but it is a part of our culture that calls for scrutiny.

At the risk of oversimplifying, I suggest that our ancestral notion of African manliness remains pervasive enough today that, despite the deaths of boys at Xhosa initiation schools in the Eastern Cape, any young man who completes his initiation in a hospital, whether for health or any other reason, risks being derided by his peers as no more than a boy, an *inkwenkwe*. No wonder some choose to die in the bush rather than suffer this humiliation.

This notion of African manhood was modelled by King Shaka on the death of his mother in 1827, when he ruthlessly commanded his subjects to pour all their milk on the ground and cease farming to show their grief – or face execution.[4] It is also showcased in Chinua Achebe's book *Things Falls*

Apart when the lead character, on hearing about a devoted elderly man who "could not do anything" without telling his wife, comments in surprise that he had thought the husband was a "strong man". Clearly, the man's willingness to share everything with his wife meant he was weak, not a "real" man.

As to the effects of this on children, I will merely point to the case of the Griekwastad farm murders in the Northern Cape[5], in which a social worker told the high court that the accused, a black boy, "had been raised not to show emotion or cry in the presence of other people".

So black African men are unable to grieve?

Black men may occasionally shed tears, but not often enough. The sense of shame and revulsion I felt all these years at the risk of allowing myself to cry can hardly be expressed here. And I know I am not the only one with a story of private trauma and unresolved grief. So it seems useful to share lessons from my struggle so that others in a similar situation can know.

Have you learnt to cry now?

I wish I could say yes. But the truth is that I have only once shed tears since I sobbed in my mother's arms as I learnt of my father's death. In 2010 I went to a club one night with my cousins during a family gathering, and got so drunk that I had to be carried home. When I heard about the incident, I felt such deep shame that tears streamed down my face while I was alone in my room. I'm sure this was partly my long-buried sadness bubbling to the surface. But I still find it hard to show emotion. Anytime I become teary, I still fight it. The fear is still there, I guess, of becoming a laughing stock by crying openly.

Did you never cry on the day of your father's funeral?

No, not even when my sister and I saw my father's coffin disappear into the earth on the day of the burial.

Did the sangomas and your family's elders say anything to comfort you?

That might have been helpful. I can't say why it didn't happen. But this is probably common in black South African communities.

Is there no indigenous procedure for consoling children in the same way that your mother was comforted at the time of your father's death?

It seems there is no precedent in my culture for comforting grieving children and encouraging them to talk about their feelings. Even at the death of Nelson Mandela, all the media attention – and there was plenty – was heaped on his widow, Graca, and to a lesser extent his ex-wife, Winnie. Little, if any, attention was directed towards the great-grandchildren. Of course, I have no way of knowing how comfort was dispersed among the Mandela family, who were comforted more than most, but the intense media focus on the past and present wife seemed to imply that the women, rather than the children, are the most fragile and in need of comfort after a loss.

And a boy child has the additional burden of trying to "be a man" while they grieve?

Yes. And this is even greater when they lose their father. I recall the death of a well-known TV presenter in this country, whose young son was among the speakers at his funeral. I don't know if this is a tradition or a new trend, but it's something I've begun to notice. The boy was so innocent, confident and articulate; clearly in stage one of the grieving process. I couldn't help wondering if he had any real understanding of what it meant to face life without a father, without the influence and support of that father–son bond.

But I am sure he felt, as all boys who lose their father must, that now he had to become the man of the house.

In my case, a male elder put this into words a few months after my father's death. Had he seen through my pained smiles and wanted to cheer me up? Did he mean that my family couldn't be expected to focus on me because my mother needed the attention? Whatever his intention, the meaning was clear. Men don't cry; they "man" the household.

I was fully aware that I was now the "father" of my family. As the eldest male child I had to set an example for my siblings, not just by not grieving, but by how I conducted myself in general. This partly explains why I went on to excel at school. If I couldn't be the man, what would they think of me?

That embrace with my mother was the only moment when my father's death brought us closer together. But it also helped to make clear what our tragedy meant to her in those early days. Even that natural and straightforward act seemed to require me to acknowledge that I must take my father's place in our family of five.

It went unspoken, but my mother's actions continued to indicate as much. She threw herself into funding my first year of university studies, and seemed the worse for wear when I saw the poverty and sacrifice she endured to do this. Later, when it became clear that Sino would be going on to tertiary studies and that my father's shoes were too big for me, she complained to a neighbour. "I thought Thabo would be the one to put Sino through university. Now I don't know what I'll do."

I recently read an account by a young black man of his own struggle after his father's death in a car accident when he was thirteen. "Relatives were more concerned about my mother's wellbeing than mine," he said. "As the eldest child, I suddenly had to step in and be 'the man' ... I wanted to alleviate my mother's pain so badly that I missed the chance to grieve."[6]

Not surprisingly, his real name was withheld. Because real men don't cry.

As a result, young black men often don't get over their trauma. I am just one example. I believe it is no coincidence that I am the one writing this memoir, not my sister or my mother. They were more able to move on after my father's death than I was. Even now, to admit that I struggled to come to terms with my father's death isn't easy.

So you feel more care needs to be taken with grieving children?

The experts point out that the grieving process for children is more complicated than for adults, because they pick up the slightest change in the emotional state of the adults they look up to. That's why a grieving parent often has a tougher time. They have to get over their loss as quickly as possible, because they have to be strong for their children too.

So perhaps having a child speak at his father's funeral is a good thing, in that it helps him to talk openly about his pain and loss. Grieving children, the experts say, should also be encouraged to ask questions, and be given honest answers. If talking isn't possible, drawing or writing is also good, as psychologists well know.

In learning about your father, did you learn anything about yourself?

I think now that part of my effort to get to know him was an attempt to discover myself. It wasn't as if I had moved to the city without my father's shadow. He had set a precedent; he had journeyed to Port Elizabeth years before me, although his motivation had been to earn, rather than to study. I knew he had lived there from a young age, but I hadn't yet grasped its significance in shaping my own life.

How appropriate it seems to me now that my father was away from home in another town on the last day of his life, and that I too was staying somewhere else on that day. He was never impressed by those who were reluctant to venture out into the world. He had always held that it was his duty to dislodge himself from his parents and stand on his own feet. I took the same view as I grew up, and saw school holidays as an opportunity to get away.

As I have come to fully grasp where the city life had taken us both, I have also had to acknowledge the similarity of my own landmarks and significant episodes during those years when I too took to smoking, drinking and womanising, and regularly lost my jobs through bad behaviour. Without knowing it, I was following in my old man's footsteps, until I too reached rock bottom and my own time of reckoning.

Thabo Jijana

Banana Moon

A sore heart brings to mind an open wound
that is the consequence
of some mishap with a Minora blade, gaping
like the corner of a reliable suitcase
torn at the seam
in some freak accident the bus conductor
forgot to tell you about
after loading your luggage,
leaving exposed some things it would do well
not to draw a stranger's eye to.
You don't want to have to explain the strip
of Elastoplast on your chin,
as though
you can't hold a shaving razor properly.
It isn't a nice thing
to befall one – yes.
It's shameful
to talk about – maybe.
Hence you laugh it away
much like when you clutch your belongings
tight under the armpit,
making light of the conductor's crime
long after you've gotten off the bus.

To see this story better, close your eyes
and picture a mud village
safely hidden in a quiet valley.

Nobody's Business

There is the sort of beat-up sedan
that passes for a short-distance taxicab
they call *iphela*
in black townships
parked near the kraal;
it is late one Saturday evening,
and now a banana of a moon
casts a cloak of dim light
over the proceedings

– that takes care of the "Where?"

The "What?" is the thing that took place
on the heels of auntie Nokwakha's funeral,
where I remember seeing uncle Mncedi weep
and laugh
just a little
in front of a tentful of attendees,
stopping every now and then
to wipe his tears
with a handkerchief
some alert female mourner upfront
had gotten off her chair and handed him.
The first time
in my twenty-odd years
I had seen uncle Mncedi –
a keen public speaker
and reigning champ
for best dining-room raconteur

among my people –
lose his composure;
The only time
I would ever see a man of my family
conduct himself
this way.

When? How? Why? Forget all that.

I won't say my cousins weren't having fun,
the five of them piled into Nyaniso's jalopy,
to each man his own glass.
It was there, I suspect, that they carried out
their aftertears,
a tipplers' caucus
on a cold August.

I was the "Who?" this night – the omission.
Too young with the bottle. No *vrou*.
So I hung back.

This was before I had matured enough
to detest the modern black funeral
for how it is treated as though
it were another traditional ceremony:
comparable only
to a lavish birthday party
with a guest of honour
whose presence

is only a grainy ID photo
on a piece of paper.

Before I knew Murphy's law: a supposed edict
of Mother Nature, to the effect that anything
that can go wrong
will
indeed
go wrong.

On some days
when something sets me thinking
about the night of the banana moon,
I wonder to myself
if it had occurred at all
to any of my brothers
to ask themselves
whether they drank Castle Lite
to dull their pain
or maybe,
just maybe,
they had merely acquired
a shared affection
for funerals
the way some people
love public holidays
in this nation of ours:
for the festive vigils
that go on and on

Thabo Jijana

    and on and on
    and on and on
    past the burial
    at the local tavern?

Twelve

ALL THE TIME THAT I REMAINED IGNORANT of my father's past, I didn't care about what I didn't know. But this quickly changed once my relatives had shared their anecdotes.

Getting to know my father's story – his humble beginnings; my grandparents' struggle to get him to school; their poverty; his marriage to my mother and the life he tried to make for us; the setbacks; and finally the upliftment his taxi job had promised – was like reading an epic in which the hero always has a fighting chance. All along, everyone keeps rooting for the hero to make it in the end, to find his pot of gold and return to build his castle.

Only in this story, the hero is only in his forties when he dies, without ever reaching the gold. His struggles had proved futile, and all that remained was our pain.

I felt cheated. I felt angry. Why did his life have to end the way it did?

People die in the most painful ways, certainly. Yet to have lost my father through an incident that was so easily preventable felt unbearable. In 2008, when children died in poorly constructed schools after the earthquake in Sichuan, China, there were naturally screams and howls about the unfairness of it. The same occurred after the 2013 factory collapse in Dhaka, Bangladesh.

So who could blame me for my anguish at the unreasonableness of my father's demise – a poor man meeting his death while striving to protect the only means he knew of making an honest living?

Questions that had always niggled me now began to take on a new urgency. What had really happened that day? And why? Who actually killed my father? And where was this person now?

Although I had wondered about these things, I had never been ready to hear the answers. Now I felt that if I didn't find out, I would regret it for the rest of my life.

At the time of my father's funeral, it had not occurred to me to raise any questions once his colleague had explained the cause of his death. I accepted that it was a stakeout gone horribly wrong and left it at that. But now this wasn't enough to placate me. I could no longer settle for such a glib explanation. In my desperate need to make some kind of sense of his loss, I began groping for answers to explain the cruelty of what had happened.

But how could I possibly understand what went on that day without first knowing the background to the taxi violence in South Africa?

It was time for the journalist in me to get to work. I needed to understand the taxi wars that had cost my father his life.

The source of the struggle, I soon discovered, went back even before he was born.

By the mid-twentieth century, South Africa's transport industry was as racially segregated as any other sector during apartheid. Almost the only car whites would allow black people to travel in was a police van. If a *khwela-khwela* pulled up at your house and white men in uniform got out, you could look forward to a long, cold night in jail.

The Motor Carrier Transportation (MCT) Act, introduced by the Hertzog government in 1930 and still in force, stipulated that all taxis required a permit. With the *dompas* already making life difficult for blacks, obtaining a permit for a black taxi owner was no easy process.

First, black operators had to be evaluated as citizens. They had to produce documents to show that they had a good formal employment record, had lived in the relevant magisterial district as legally registered tenants for a number of years and had a Daily Labourer's Permit.

Even if they met all these requirements, the quota system allowed only a few permits to be issued each year. And even then, the MCT Act only authorised the use of small cars carrying no more than four passengers. The system was totally illogical, given the sea of black commuters forced to live outside the city and travel great distances to work each day. By design, the MCT Act limited the transport market to white-controlled buses and trains. Now at last I understood why black people in short stories prior to the 1970s never used taxis.

Inevitably, many black taxis began operating illegally, using private saloon cars to transport passengers.

By the late 1980s, apartheid was becoming a big headache for the white government, which began trying all sorts of ways to appease a black population ready to die for its liberation. It decided at this point to allow some of the angry mob into the traditionally all-white economy, by setting up, for example, dummy township councils that only exacerbated the situation.

In 1987, the government also saw fit to cease regulating the transportation industry and welcome previously excluded black people who may have wanted to participate in the country's taxi industry but were denied access under the old laws.

That was the magical year in which the government officially opened the gates for entry into the transportation industry. Virtually overnight, the taxi industry became a hugely popular sector among blacks. It was welcomed by both taxi operators, who could legally enter the system for the first time, and commuters, who were happy to switch from buses and trains, which were time-consuming, perilous and expensive.

The Toyota HiAce minibus became the signature model for the taxi industry, and was quickly nicknamed the Zola

Budd – after South Africa's Olympic runner, who Brenda Fassie immortalised in a song.

The South African Black Taxi Association, SABTA, which had existed before deregulation, now assumed far greater authority. In an effort to unify the hundreds of new taxi associations cropping up at a furious rate all around the country, it began organising them into local, regional and provincial clusters.

But with vast amounts of money to be made, it wasn't long before rifts began to develop, as taxi alliances formed and then split with alarming frequency. And soon the first of the "taxi wars" broke out.

After democracy, SABTA morphed into the South African National Taxi Council, better known as Santaco. But the violence, rather than abating after the fall of apartheid, only intensified.

In the highly aggressive but minimally policed world of South Africa's taxi industry, it is no surprise that trust was rare. Money was the only currency in this business, and alliances were driven less by regional or provincial bonds than by efforts to achieve supremacy over routes. It was Taxi Business 101: make friends, make enemies. What counted was who could make you the most money for the least trouble. In consequence, each town typically had several taxi associations, some allied to bigger groups and others not, with some heavily reliant on their mother body, while others were only nominally aligned.

As groups continually coalesced and splintered, association members regularly turned on one another in leadership struggles. Truces between warring factions rarely held for long – an indication, if ever one was needed, that violence was probably never far from the thoughts of anyone in the driver's seat of all those thousands of taxis that took to the roads each day in South Africa.

Yet somehow, because the wars were waged by loosely allied groups with different goals, they seldom achieved a clear outcome – whether because the police finally put a stop to the proceedings or because the warring groups reached a ceasefire by themselves. Without a clear winner, each side claimed victory. Typically, a blame game about who started the fight took centre stage.

Intriguingly, in all my research into taxi violence, never once did I find the name or face of a taxi operator attached to any media story, even when suspects had been arrested and appeared in court. This seemed to be the norm for all reports of taxi violence. It was as if the details of taxi crimes were nobody's business. No wonder the public have tended to regard the taxi industry as untouchable.

At the same time, media reports gave the impression that the taxi wars involved a myriad of associations. Surely, then, it was everybody's business?

But rarely did a taxi organisation take responsibility for its crimes and vow to resolve its disputes with competitors. If the war was nobody's business, then its crimes were nobody's business either. And so it was for the war that claimed my father's life. No taxi association – let alone their leaders – ever claimed to have instigated the fight. Each side claimed to have been defending itself against the other.

Well, I wanted to be the reporter who dug deeper and found out the true reasons behind at least one fatality of the taxi wars: my father's. I wanted to write the story that put a face to the crime.

And so I began to explore the alliances behind the war that had led to my father's death.

In the Eastern Cape, the two major provincial associations were the Ncedo Taxi Association and the Border Alliance Taxi Association (Bata). Bata took its name from the "border regions" surrounding King William's Town. Originally, in the 1980s, Bata referred to operators from outside the town whose daily routes linked them to this popular shopping hub where Bata was headquartered.

The Peddie Taxi Association was a member of Bata, which offered it the upper hand over their urban rivals in King William's Town itself. In the urban area, many residents had their own cars and the distances were shorter, meaning less profitable routes for the local taxi operators, who belonged to the Bhisho-King Taxi Association, Bhikita, with its taxi rank and offices at the Market Square in the CBD. Bata preferred their taxi ranks in places that best suited the out-of-town commuters – at the local Spar, and at the petrol station where the last bus stopped on the way out of town. This helped Bata to maintain its monopoly over the long-distance commuters travelling to and from King William's Town.

Thirteen

It was early in February 2013 when I finally set out to track down the truth about how my father had died. Since dropping out of university I had tried my hand at writing and journalism. In 2011 I took an internship at a newspaper in Grahamstown. The following year I freelanced as a journalist in Port Elizabeth, but soon gave it up. Then in 2013 my luck turned, when the online magazine Mampoer selected me as one of two young writers to participate in their mentorship programme. With their financial backing, I was able to start investigation for my debut article – the story of my father's murder. As intensely personal as this story was, I tried my best to approach it with professional rigour and detachment.

The one person I was certain would have at least some of the answers to my questions was the man who had spoken at my father's funeral, Mzwandile Gwejela. So I took a trip to Peddie.

I found the old town just as I remembered it: the Engen petrol station beside the highway; the smiling children on Omo billboards beside the road. The N2 into town was undergoing roadworks and there was no likelihood that this would be finished anytime soon. Old vans ruled the streets, puffs of smoke like farts coming out of their behinds. There were too few rubbish bins on the pavements, too many streams of water running down the roads, no traffic lights in sight and the ANC was still firmly in charge. Nothing much was new.

The Peddie taxi rank was just beside the road, and there was no way to enter or leave town without passing it. Gwejela was by now the chairperson of the Peddie Taxi Association, as well as owning a fleet of taxis and running his own driving school.

One sunny Tuesday morning I arrived at his small office beside the taxi rank. I had not made an appointment, but I had deliberately timed my visit midweek, taking care to avoid paydays or pension day which always make a taxi rank busier. Payday fell on the fifteenth of the month for state nurses, the twentieth for teachers, the twenty-fifth for municipal workers and other state employees, and at month-end for policemen and the rest of the workforce. Pension day was the first of the month for those on the new social grant system, but varied by village for those who still received their money the old way, at specialised pay points supplied by a cash-in-transit vehicle.

Despite my best effort to choose a good day, I found that Gwejela wasn't alone.

My unannounced stopover had unfortunately coincided with a *stokvel* executive meeting, and three of his colleagues sat in metal chairs, their attention directed at the table where Gwejela – a squat, bespectacled man – and a secretary stood counting cash. As each money bag was emptied onto the table, one taxi owner would shout out the amount and a name, so that whoever the cash belonged to could be noted down in a book.

"Another R500!"

"That's from Mkhontwana."

"How much is that now?"

"R2 000."

"No, it's R2 500."

I told Gwejela that I wanted to speak to him about my father's death.

My request was not received warmly. It was obvious that he would prefer not to talk about it.

"Show me your ID," he said brusquely. "Prove that you are who you say you are." It was clear that he didn't trust me.

I took it out and gave it to him. Standing and leaning on his office desk before me, Gwejela was obviously in two minds, pulled between the meeting he was presiding over and my request for an interview.

I took a chair and waited patiently. Inside the crowded office, files and ledgers were stacked halfway up one wall and piled on top of overstuffed cabinets. The claustrophobic feel of slightly outdated industrialism was relieved only by a lone, knee-high pot plant in one corner and a PC on the table. Tacked to the wall near my seat was a calendar that had been turned around, and on its bare, white surface were listed the names of ninety or so taxi owners who operated from the Peddie taxi rank.

I had taken a seat by the open door, through which I could see life in full cry. From the hawkers' caravans, plates of rice, chicken or beef were being sold. Fruit and vegetable stands consisted of old school desks with cardboard table tops. The offices of the taxi rank were situated in a block of flats, and if there were toilets, they evidently weren't working, since men were dashing to the adjacent shrubs to pee, while the women were forced to pay a fee to use the restrooms at the Engen petrol station. The air was filled with odours – cooking smells, car fumes, the stench of decaying rubbish and a putrid stream – amid the loud babble of voices from the people milling around.

Peddie had been the subject of the SABC1 drama *Tsha-Tsha*, and its dire shortage of jobs for young people was representative of the national norm. Here they were making money any way they could – by pushing a wheelbarrow for *gogos* who couldn't carry their groceries to the taxi, working in hair salons, selling shrivelled fruit at the taxi rank, or hawking cheap merchandise such as pirated CDs, dishcloths, nail-clippers or cockroach poison.

As I waited for Gwejela to grant me an interview, I looked back at the men counting their cash, and the words of a former transport minister came into my mind.

> *The taxi industry, which is black-owned, controlled and run, cannot forever remain at the margins in economic terms. The taxi industry is a key player in the economy of our country.*[7]

Much as I understood the capitalist ambitions that had brought Gwejela and the other men into the taxi industry, I wanted to understand what drove them to so often settle their disputes through the bullet. This was the line of questioning I had prepared for Gwejela.

I should have expected some stonewalling, I began to realise. This was, after all, the most violent industry in the country, and talk of old grudges could be enough to get you killed. I had naïvely assumed that being the son of a late colleague would ease things. But I wasn't prepared to give up, so I waited as though I had the whole day, even though I didn't.

Gwejela finally turned from his huddle of compatriots to look at me.

"Come again tomorrow," he said.

I thought I hadn't heard him correctly.

He was prepared to talk the next day, he said, only when he'd heard from my mother that she endorsed my visit.

"I had hoped to talk now," I said, unable to hide my disappointment. I had a long list of other places to visit and I was short on time. "I'll call my mother now," I pleaded.

"Don't push it." He was growing impatient. "Do as I say and I'll help you."

Now I was distrustful too. I was afraid I wouldn't find him in his office the next day and that I'd have to chase him around to get answers. At that moment I didn't care that the money he was counting mattered more to him than my problems. Maybe I had come across just like one of the young taxi drivers who show no respect for their betters. Or was it part of the discipline of an experienced taxi driver that the less an outsider knew about the taxi wars, the less risk he was to the taxi operators involved? This was a matter of safety and security, after all, and the less said, the better.

"I won't take much of your time," I heard myself protest.

"I don't think you're hearing me," Gwejela said. He meant this as an expression of incredulity. "Come back tomorrow."

I got up and Gwejela resumed counting the money.

"Okay," I said. "See you tomorrow."

"Okay," he said.

That night I slept at auntie Nolwandle's house. The house had seen some serious renovations since a decade ago, and now had a private bedroom for auntie as well as two others. I went to her room and we talked about that time when I was holidaying with her family. There were still so many things I didn't know about her that one normally knows about a family member, and I discarded my shyness to ask her.

How had she come to own a house in Peddie, I wanted to know. She said that after her father Mpukwana got fired from his job in kwaKerry, they all went to live on another farm nearer to town. A few years later they moved to a village, and in his last years they moved once more to another village, all close to town. Why so much moving? She supposed that he was looking for work and a better life. And why had she then relocated the family to Peddie? As the oldest daughter when her father died in the 1970s, she explained, she had to find work, and Peddie seemed a good place to start. When did she start selling fruit and fish in town? After she arrived in Peddie in 1979. How many siblings did she have? Five. Wasn't there an older brother, besides the one I knew who also lived in Peddie Extension? Yes, but he went to Johannesburg to find work, just like uncle/*bawomkhulu* Mncedi and uncle Xhantilomzi – and sometimes didn't return for decades. "That's why you barely know him. I hardly hear from him myself."

Had she ever been married? Yes, once, she said. But she got divorced a long time ago. Was her ex-husband still alive? No, he had died in 2010.

At last I reminded her about the episode I had witnessed the night before I left for my home village to discover that my father had died.

"What happened that evening?" I asked her.

She said she'd had an average day at her vendor's stand in town, and when the sun went down she packed up and found a taxi. Apart from the driver, she didn't know the other commuters well and could barely recall who they were, except for a very talkative young woman in the front seat who she knew by association. "She just couldn't stop talking," auntie said.

When the car had almost reached auntie's stop, the woman in the front seat said, "What a sad thing that happened to that man."

Auntie asked what the story was.

"The man who was killed," the woman said, "In King William's Town. The taxi driver."

"What taxi driver?"

"Mzalwane. Don't you know him? That's what they call him."

At first auntie didn't make the connection. Then the woman told her that his surname was Jijana.

As she suddenly grasped the full implications of what the woman was saying, something welled up in her chest. She was having a panic attack.

"It was like I needed air," she said. "I had to get out of the car."

The taxi stopped. She got out. Two of the commuters volunteered to help her to the house. Once she got there the adults in the house tried to console her, but she was so distraught that they could do very little. During the night one of my cousins relayed a message to uncle Vuyani about my father's death. They needed to decide what to do about me, his fifteen-year-old son who was staying with them.

"My heart problems got worse after that," auntie told me. "I've never been the same."

Fourteen

THE FOLLOWING MORNING I gathered all my courage and set out for the taxi rank to face Gwejela again. I felt suddenly acutely conscious of myself as a paler shade of my father. I had something of his look about me – how could I not? – I got nervous in crowds, I didn't let my hair grow more than a cropped afro, I hated fighting, I loved good music, and I was continuously revising my personality. I was also aware of my tendency to mess up my isiXhosa at times, since imported American culture had turned my entire Generation Facebook into coconuts without us realising it.

But the unruffled young man who walked into Gwejela's office that Wednesday in a black blazer and chinos with matching shoes had a spoonful of his old man's courage in him – quiet as he was, this was a man who didn't like being messed around.

I had come to back to get the answers I felt entitled to.

Gwejela sat on a chair in front of me this time. He was prepared to talk to me. He was well dressed in a crisp shirt and expensive shoes. At first glance he appeared modest, but beneath his restraint I sensed a powerful ego. I wasn't sure if I could trust him.

"How did the war start that claimed my father's life?" I wanted to know.

In contrast to the previous day, he was less guarded and more talkative.

"The trouble began," he said, "with a letter from the King William's Town municipality in 2000. It said that all taxi associations operating across town had to come together and operate from one central site."

"Why would the municipality do that?" I asked.

Gwejela looked at me for a brief moment as I spoke, and then turned to stare into the world outside his open door with a distant look as he answered.

"We were told it was the government's plan that every town should have one central taxi rank. To unify the industry."

Taxi bosses across town saw this as a potential return to the "dark days" of government regulation prior to 1987, and were deeply distrustful of the municipality's decree. Each association wanted to protect its hard-won travelling routes and standing in the community, and their biggest worry, Gwejela said, was that they might lose out to other operators.

And there was now the question of who would get the best positions at the central taxi rank.

The municipal letter came with an added directive. All associations working in King William's Town had to be part of an existing local taxi forum. Bata's competitors, the Ncedo or Bhikita Taxi Associations, were already part of the local forum, but Bata wasn't.

"What did all this have to do with my father?" I wanted to know.

"Our Peddie Taxi Association was affiliated to Bata," he reminded me. "It is an old fight between us and them." He was referring to Bhikita's bitterness over Bata's domination of the most lucrative sector of the King William's Town market.

In essence, the letter said that Bata and Bhikita would have to work together and share the market. Bata would have to relocate while Bhikita would not. It wasn't a request. It was a command.

Bata grudgingly consented, as they were legally compelled to. But they were bitter at being left out of the discussions that favoured a single central taxi rank and declared Bata's ranks illegal. And they were incensed that it would result in a loss of market share to Bhikita.

Their relocation to the Market Square happened gradually over a year or more. As a cautionary step, the police instituted a ban on all weapons, Gwejela told me. By 2002, everything seemed to be in order.

And that's when the trouble really began.

The war had started with some harmless intimidation – men feeling each other out, as they say. Then ugly words were exchanged. Soon these became threats, and isolated fights broke out. Some drivers managed to smuggle knobkerries, Okapis and stones into the taxi rank, which caused some injuries. Tensions continued to escalate, and one day a minibus taxi was set alight.

All the time Gwejela was speaking, I was holding my emotions in check, forcing myself to listen as a journalist. Mentally I ticked off each question as he answered it, while furiously scribbling down new questions to ask.

"But how did my father even end up in King William's Town?" I asked him now.

Until then, he said, the fight had been between the Bata and Bhikita taxi operators based in King William's Town. But as hostilities intensified, the taxi associations began bullying and provoking one another, which extended the battle beyond King William's Town to involve their alliance partners. As each tried to poach the others' customers, quasi no-go areas developed for one association or another, and – as the main area of contention – each group felt the need to safeguard their space at the Market Square taxi rank.

Each and every association member, from all of Bata's and Bhikita's alliances, was allocated shifts during which they would be on watch duty, covering most, if not all, of their association's space. The result was that the Market Square taxi rank was occupied twenty-four hours a day. Taxis full of operators travelled in from as far as two hours away for their shifts.

I reminded Gwejela of what he had said at the funeral, and asked him to tell me how my father died.

My father had driven alone, he said, to Gwejela's office in Peddie just after midnight, which would have taken him about half an hour. From there they all left together in one taxi – my father, Gwejela, Madodana, Ntlontlo and seven others – for King William's Town, to begin their shift in the early hours of Friday morning.

"How were they dressed?" I asked.

"Warmly. Heavy jackets, woollen beanies, balaclavas."

The journey to King William's Town would have taken no more than forty minutes with so little traffic on the N2 at that hour. Once they reached Market Square, there wasn't much to do.

"We sat inside the van talking, drinking coffee and smoking," said Gwejela.

At sunrise the rank began to fill up. They were still lounging around in the van when the first rocks showered their car.

"Someone shouted that we were being attacked," he said. "We were totally surprised, and tried to escape from the taxi as quick as we could." But there was no plan, no coordination in their frantic escape.

"We got separated," he explained. "Three of us ran down and took shelter at a small takeaway store. Others ran to the Engen garage where there was still a Bata rank. We didn't stop to think. We just ran for our lives."

A mob was upon them. "We lost sight of each other, and I didn't know who went where. I almost didn't make it myself," Gwejela went on. "If the owner hadn't locked the doors after we came in, we wouldn't have been saved from our attackers."

"But your father got separated," Gwejela said, his voice betraying emotion. "Once out of the van he ran his own way."

I pictured my father, all alone in the midst of the chaos. "We waited. Thirty minutes, an hour, maybe more, wondering what had happened and where the others were. We were still hiding in the shop when I got a call on my cell phone," Gwejela said. "They said one of our own had been hit."

Soon after that call, they were told it was safe to come out. The body, they were told, was a little beyond where they had been hiding, nearer to Bhikita's office on the western end of the taxi rank.

"When we got there we could see someone lying dead on the ground." He sighed. "It was your father."

"And do you know who killed him?"

"No."

There was a moment of silence. Throughout our conversation his eyes had rarely met mine, and I couldn't help wondering if he was withholding information. My questions began to grow more blunt, even hostile.

"You have no idea what happened to my father after you were separated from him during the attack?"

"No, I don't."

"Was anyone ever arrested?"

"I don't know. Have you spoken to the police?"

I shook my head.

"You should."

I left Gwejela's office with mixed feelings. I was relieved that he had spoken to me, but I had been hoping for more.

Outside Gwejela's office I found two of my father's other

colleagues from the Peddie Taxi Association, who had also been with my father on that fateful watch in King William's Town. As we stood talking under a billboard on the western side of the rank, I learnt a little more from them.

"Those Bhikita drivers," Mawabo Ntlontlo told me, "the ones who had loading bays in front of ours, would position their taxis so we couldn't get out of the rank. What could we do but respond the same way?"

"During the day," Mzameni Madodana said, "we would see the Bhikita people carrying bags of potatoes to their offices. We didn't know that once inside, the bags were being emptied of potatoes and filled with rocks. Whenever there was a confrontation, the rocks were emptied onto the pavement in front of their offices, so any one of them could easily pick up a rock and hurl it at us."

"How big were these rocks? I asked him.

"Big," he said.

"Would you say they intended to cause you injuries?" I wondered.

"They meant to kill us."

"Or maybe – "

"That was their only intention."

"I see. Do you know where I can find any of the others who were with him on that last day?"

They pointed to two men sitting beside a food vendor's caravan, waiting their turn to load their taxis with commuters and head out.

I went over and greeted them loudly, explaining that I was a journalist and what I wanted to know. They were instantly wary. Although they admitted that they had been with my father that day, they refused to say more. Knowing that I was a journalist, they clearly feared repercussions if their names became linked to taxi warfare.

I felt combative, suspecting that they might be concealing something. But I was growing used to this reticence among taxi drivers at the first mention of taxi violence.

Fifteen

VERY EARLY ONE FRIDAY MORNING in February 2013, I boarded a taxi in Peddie for King William's Town. Although the journey was less than an hour, I had to wait for over an hour for the taxi to fill up before we could leave. But I didn't mind. It gave me time to consider what I had learnt so far, and what I planned to do next.

I now knew a bit more about how my father had died. I had hoped this would be enough, but I still wasn't satisfied. The story felt unfinished.

My old sense of injustice at my father's loss had returned. How could it not? My father had been murdered, after all. And what exactly had been done about it? I wanted to speak to someone on the other side, to get a balanced story. But most of all I wanted to hear from the police.

As I waited in the taxi, I reflected on the state of the industry. It had changed immensely since the old days. With the benefit of hindsight, much as deregulation was a step in the right direction, it had also thrown the taxi industry into disarray. The old guidelines applied by the apartheid regime, although designed to keep blacks out of the industry, had at least maintained order. Suddenly they were abandoned without being replaced by equally strict rules. In a sense, the government simply stopped policing the industry.

As one taxi operator put it, "They deregulated it without ever regulating it."[8]

Overnight it became a free for all. Too many taxi owners entered the industry far too quickly, including a mass of unlicenced operators. Illegal taxi ranks flourished. If the government wouldn't regulate the taxi bosses, they would have do it themselves. Once the taxi associations were up and running, they took the role of informal self-regulators. And many used exploitation and coercion to build lucrative empires-cum-protection-rackets. These were also directly associated with the violence that had plagued the taxi industry from its early days.[9]

Since then, South Africa had become a democracy, the Truth and Reconciliation Commission had run its course, twenty years of democracy had unfolded, and women had joined the ranks of taxi drivers. Yet the government's response to taxi violence had not improved.

The taxi industry had rapidly surpassed trains and buses to

account for a whopping sixty per cent of the total commuter market. Thousands of minibus taxis ply our country's roads daily, contributing billions to South Africa's GDP. Yet at the time of going to press, the government has only barely begun a few tentative and poorly enforced measures to transform this pivotal industry into a fully professional sector of the formal economy.

The government's belated attempts to regulate the industry have proved no easy ride, with fierce resistance to all forms of government intervention. The industry has gained such a bad reputation for its brazen disregard of road rules – unroadworthy vehicles overloaded with passengers – that the prime focus of government action has been road safety. Millions have now been invested in a national transport academy[10] aimed to improve road safety and driver skills.

Yet calls remain for a complete overhaul of the transport industry. After years of trying to negotiate with taxi bosses, the government seemed to have decided to go it alone, despite continued opposition to its efforts. The Bus and Rapid Transit system (BRT), also known as the Integrated Public Transport Network and System (IPTS), aims to integrate different forms of transport on specific routes so that commuters can use a single ticket to cover both taxi and bus travel on a single long trip. This is intended to minimise road congestion by limiting taxis to points outside of city centres and using buses for trips inside the CBD.

It seems inevitable that more fighting will break out.[11]

When I reached King William's Town, my first stop was the local Spar in the CBD, where there was once a Bata street rank.

I wanted to know whether the Spar owners felt things had changed since the old Bhikita–Bata war. I spoke to one of the general managers, a middle-aged man with a thick moustache who invited me into his office. Like most people I spoke to, he didn't want his name revealed for fear of repercussions.

"It was like a war zone," he told me, betraying no sign of exaggeration. "The Bhikita people would be on one side of the street and the Bata people on the other side, all firing at one another with AK-47s."[12]

"Are things any different now?" I asked.

"It's been quiet," he replied.

He couldn't specifically remember the 2003 taxi war. "There were so many, my friend, it's hard to keep count," he said.

Next I decided to visit the Bhikita offices in the centre of town. "They love fighting," Gwejela had said of Bhikita. I was hoping that Tutu Zicina, the chairperson of the King William's Town Taxi Forum and a Bhikita taxi boss, could shed more light on the events surrounding my father's death.

Zicina turned out to be a surprisingly pleasant character, far from the tough-guy type I had been led to expect. But he couldn't tell me much.

"When did the violence you talk about take place?" he asked. My answer drew an exclamation of surprise. "Forgive me, but that's a long time ago. I don't remember it at all."

I asked if my description of the events on that day sounded plausible.

"Yes," he said. "There was a lot of violence during that time."

I mentioned the potato bags full of rocks. Was it true?

"I'm not too sure about that," he said, "but I can't say it didn't happen."

"Which of the two organisations was to blame?" I asked.

"There's no way to say," he told me, acknowledging that Bhikita and its affiliates were as guilty as Bata. "We both did the same things."

About a year after my father's death, he told me, by which time several more taxi drivers had been killed, the two associations called a meeting and agreed not to integrate their taxi ranks after all.

It came as a shock to realise that my father had lost his life because of a foolish experiment that had failed. The futility of it made it even harder to bear. It might have been some small comfort to know that his death had influenced the decision to revert to separate ranks. But as always, it was economic interest rather than the safety of the drivers and passengers that ultimately decided the matter. The fighting was losing both sides too much money.

Finally I asked Zicina about the status quo. He assured me that the taxi war between Bata and Bhikita was over.

"But those people at Bata," he added, "they don't want to listen. Every town has a taxi forum, and all the taxi associations that work there must belong to it. But Bata doesn't belong to ours. They don't want to share routes. When our taxis go to other towns in the Transkei or their taxis come here, we accommodate each other. We allow them to operate in our rank, just as they do when we visit their towns. But Bata doesn't want to do this. They want to operate by themselves."

The old rivalry between Bata and Bhikita clearly hadn't gone away. I couldn't help wondering how long the peace would hold.

I visited the owner of the small takeaway store near Zicina's office, and asked how things had ended after the shooting in July 2003. His first response, inevitably, was fear. He would only speak to me after I assured him he wouldn't end up in court as a result.

"Okay then," he said. "What do you want to know?"

I told him about my father's death at the taxi rank in 2003.

"I can't remember that far back," he said. "There have been lots of taxi wars here." Each time, he said, his shop was damaged. "The taxi drivers would chase each other and some would run in here. If the others saw them inside, they would try to force their way in, so I always locked my doors. When they couldn't break the bars to get in, they would break my windows with stones. While the drivers were hiding here their taxis would be attacked. We heard the windows being smashed with knobkerries and the tyres slashed. The situation would be bad for months until the police put a stop to it."

Finally I headed for the visit I had been dreading the most – the King William's Town police station, just off the CBD. What if, after all this effort, I didn't like what I found out from them?

I began to have doubts about the motivation behind my quest. A decade had passed since my father's death. Why did I want to know if anyone was arrested? Did I really want to confront my father's killer? It was only now beginning to occur to me that meddling in the murky underworld of the taxi wars might put my own life in danger.

But it was too late now, I decided. I wasn't one to chicken out easily.

The police station was a collection of two-storey buildings next to Healdtown FET college. I waited my turn at the reception desk. When I explained my enquiry, a policeman pointed me towards the investigations' department, where I repeated my story to a policewoman.

"Hi, my name is Thabo Jijana. I'm a journalist writing a story about a taxi murder that occurred at the taxi rank here. The person killed was my father. I want to know how he died, and if anyone was arrested."

She was willing to help. Could I give her the case number? I shook my head. "I don't have a case number."

The reason was simple. The police had never contacted my family about my father's death. During any criminal investigation, the investigating officer must provide the victim or the victim's family with a case number, which is then used for future reference to provide the family with updates about any arrests or court appearances. This had never happened.

She asked for my father's legal name. When this didn't yield any results, she asked for his date of death.

"The first week of July of 2003," I told her.

Still nothing. At this point she gave up. A policeman in the room suggested I try their colleague, who worked more closely with the archives department.

But by then it was lunchtime and the officer was out of his office. So I waited on a bench. When at last he returned I told him my tale. Despite all the data I was able to provide, he too seemed to draw a blank. Then, without a word, he went into the office next door and returned with a brown file.

I could see my father's name on the cover of the docket.

Wanting to smoke, he asked if we could go outside.

"Sure," I said.

I felt a rush of elation as we stepped out into the sunshine. At last all the documentation about my father's death was within reach. My fears of what it might contain were instantly forgotten.

The officer read the docket silently and then looked up. "The case never went to court," he told me. "No one was ever arrested."

"Okay," I said. "How do I get a copy of this document?"

He was clearly taken aback. "You can't," he said. "The law doesn't allow it."

"But I want to see it for myself."

He repeated himself. There was more talk in this fashion without me getting anywhere near the docket. Finally he suggested, rather half-heartedly, that I ask the station commander. "Look for Colonel Hobane. Maybe he'll help you."

Colonel Hobane's office was in the same corridor. As I walked in, I recognised him as the policeman I had asked for directions earlier. He cut the figure of a school principal: bald with spectacles and a considerable paunch.

Perhaps I came across as a private investigator asking for special privileges, because I had barely begun when he interrupted me.

"We can't allow you to read police dockets," he said flatly.

"Is there no other way I can gain access to the docket?" I pleaded.

"No," he said, a little grey in the face.

The disappointment on my face only sharpened his annoyance. "Are you a policeman?" he demanded.

"No," I replied.

"Then we can't allow you to read police dockets."

I lingered for a moment, in the hope that he might soften. When he didn't, I tried a final appeal.

"You've been told what happened," he said firmly. "No one was arrested. The case is still open." As I reached for the door, he added, "If we get new information, we'll tell you."

But he hadn't taken down my contact details, and he didn't ask for them.

It was difficult to swallow my disappointment as I left the police station. It was as though the gate I had struggled so hard to approach had been rudely slammed in my face. Reading an official account of my father's death would have made the incident much more real for me, and so easier to accept. The actual events surrounding his death still remained the sketchiest page in the book of memories I had started to gather about him.

As I left the police station I felt I had been unnecessarily thwarted. Perhaps I should have made it clear that I wasn't after revenge, just the official truth about my father's death. Or perhaps my father's death *was* nobody's business – Hobane evidently saw no reason to help me at all. But I had made it my business to hear the police account, and his total lack of interest in my request was a harsh blow.

I could only imagine the experiences of all the other victims of taxi violence who must have walked into police stations across the country, hoping to learn the details surrounding the death of their loved ones. "Taxi violence" was too convenient a rationale. There were real reasons beyond this vague label. Somebody had loaded the gun, taken aim and pulled the trigger. There was more to this story.

I could have simply approached the police spokesperson, as journalists routinely do, to seek favourable treatment in getting help from authorities. But I had wanted to know how it felt for the man in the street – most of whom have no concept of the perks of a journalist – to confront our country's justice system.

Anger and disappointment ping-ponged through my head as I left the police station. Hobane's attitude recalled the contemptuous black policemen of the apartheid era, now stock characters of black literature, identifiable by their steadfast apathy towards members of the public.

As I stood outside, I reflected on the initial resistance I had received from Gwejela. And my stubbornness kicked in. As unsettling as the meeting with Hobane had been, I had come too far to give up now. Knowing what I knew, I had a responsibility to act. How could I get on with my life knowing there might have been some misconduct on the part of the police or some other official that Hobane had prevented me from knowing?

One way or another, I was determined to find out how my father died. And Colonel Hobane was not going to stand in my way.

Sixteen

THREE MONTHS LATER, I was ready for another visit to King William's Town police station. But first I decided to spend the weekend with uncle/*bawomkhulu* Mncedi in the village of Ngcabasa nearby. It was getting late as the roads grew narrower and more rural as dusk approached. After winding past mountainside villages for an hour, I stepped off near a village high school and had no trouble reaching uncle/*bawomkhulu*'s four-building home, shared only by his unmarried son, my cousin Sakhele.

Uncle/*bawomkhulu* Mncedi was now a widower in his seventies, with a weakness for cricket and betting on horses. As our family historian, he could recall the details of events no other family member would think to keep note of.

"When did my father go to initiation school?" I asked him now.

"Sometime during the 1970s," he replied, "while he was working in Port Elizabeth."

This left me with food for thought. So my father had had to save up the money himself, and then presumably quit his job to spend the required month or so secluded in the bush.

That Monday morning as I set out for King William's Town, uncle/*bawomkhulu* Mncedi accompanied me, having errands of his own to do.

Millions of South Africans, I reflected – including myself and uncle/*bawomkhulu* Mncedi – used taxis every day, despite the dangers we read about in newspaper reports. Passengers had sometimes died as a result, from bullets meant for the driver. Yet I was so used to travelling in taxis that even when there was a taxi strike, my intense dislike of the industry never overcame my reliance on it. As with Eskom and South Africa's political parties, I had a strong love–hate relationship with taxis. But for some South Africans the scales had shifted, and they were considering alternatives. On the roads leaving any town or city, the chances are there is now a hitchhikers' spot somewhere there.

It wasn't rare to hear of a relative who had forsaken taxis entirely to hitchhike instead, which was also cheaper. And as motorists were struggling to keep up with petrol prices, they were increasingly likely to stop for a raised thumb on the roadside.

But taxi drivers had caught up. They had taken to keeping

vigil on hitchhikers' spots and discouraging hitchhikers from boarding non-taxis, sometime gently, often rudely, as well as threatening private motorists who stop for hitchhikers. No one ever mentioned the law in these dealings, because what would it help? On all sides, it was only the brave who took their chances. This was a growing trend that no one was speaking about.

Taxis, I reflected, were actually becoming more expensive than buses and trains if you balanced distance and reliability, although taxis still came out tops for convenience and comfort, particularly since the introduction of the Quantum taxis, which didn't come cheap. Still, a lot of South Africans still depended on taxis, and rued it greatly when there were none at the local rank.

My uncle and I parted ways, and I drew myself up to full height before entering King William's Town police station.

"I was here some months ago," I reminded Hobane, having cornered him in the corridor.

The intervening months had not mellowed the colonel. It didn't take him long to remember me as I ran through my old routine.

"My name is Thabo Jijana. I am a journalist ..."

"As we told you before," he replied, ever the implacable enemy, "you cannot view a police docket."

"But I was told to come in here."

"By who?"

I explained that the provincial SAPS spokesperson, Sibongile Soci, had advised me to file a PAIA request form at the King William's Town police station.

Following my initial visit to the police station, I had made enquiries about how to pry a document out of the grip of unhelpful authorities. And I had discovered a watershed piece of legislation in post-apartheid South Africa, which I find almost as impressive as the Truth and Reconciliation Commission. The Promotion of Access to Information Act of 2000 aims to end "the secrecy and silence" that characterised the apartheid years. It means that now, in a nation whose people have not entirely lost their mistrust of the state, an ordinary citizen can walk into any government department and file a PAIA request to access a state document. If the request is denied, there is recourse both within that department and beyond it.

But the PAIA is not without flaws, as Fola Adeleke of the South African Human Rights Commission had explained to me. The procedure can be bureaucratic and the fee prohibitive, and there is a thirty-day wait even when the information is needed urgently. I was also told that Colonel Hobane's reaction wasn't unusual. The biggest challenge to this legislation was the lack of awareness in government departments of their obligation to comply.

"Well," Hobane said evenly, "you should have come with a letter from your lawyer."

"I don't need a lawyer." I repeated what Soci had told me.

"That's not how we do it," he said.

Hobane's hostility brought to mind the rumours I had heard about police involvement in taxi violence and in hired murder. Zicina of Bhikita had told me that although police officers weren't allowed to own taxis, they sometimes registered their spouses as owners. This made me uneasy, knowing that the taxi violence was still simmering.[13] At any other time I might have backed down, but by now I was utterly determined that Hobane would not keep from me what I was entitled to know.

"You do know there's a law that says I can see police dockets?" I asked, my irritation beginning to show.

"As I said, we cannot allow you to read police dockets."

I told him about the law, but he wasn't even listening. "I've come to file a PAIA request," I concluded.

He ignored me.

"So will you go on record then as saying that you won't give me the form?" My tone was now hostile.

"I am telling you, you cannot view police dockets."

We continued in this manner, until at last he gave in. I could contact Soci, he said, and he would listen to what she had to say. He went into his office while I put a call through to Soci.

Soci was off duty. I was told I should ask Hobane to call her. But Hobane had gone out for lunch by now, and I would have to wait until 2 pm to talk to him.

I spent the lunch break thinking of how best to continue. I feared that leaving it to Hobane to make the phone call might be a dead end. So I decided to approach the SAPS spokesperson for King William's Town, Lieutenant Siphokazi Mawisa.

Mawisa phoned Hobane to verify my story before agreeing to help me. Then she advised me of the best way to submit the PAIA form, which I did the following day. Thankfully, by applying as a citizen rather than a journalist, I could avoid the fee.

Finally I left for the taxi rank in town.

Seventeen

As I waited for my PAIA request to be processed, I continued my search for answers.

In March, I decided to pay a visit to the home of the leader of my parents' church in Peddie, seven villages away from Prudhoe. Reverend Rhobo had passed away in 2004, and his seventy-year-old widow Nophumzile had assumed leadership of the Nyeleni branch.

On my way to visit her I bumped into her youngest daughter Nozibongo in town, who showed me the way there with a look of concern and pity. The two of us had known each other since childhood, having met at our parents' church. So when I explained why I wanted to visit her mother,

Nozibongo saw no need to censor her thoughts.

"What happened to your father wasn't nice," she said with a worried look. "Please find a job somewhere else," she urged me, "not in the taxi business."

My investigations elicited many such responses. Everybody had something to say about the taxi violence, some of it thoughtful, some of it poorly informed, some of it spot on. It was also interesting how people received my enquiries. Some wanted money for their time, some wanted anonymity, and others would have nothing at all to do with my investigation.

When I sat down with Nophumzile she told me about my father's baptism in Cape Town, my parents' participation in the church choir, and how happily Thabisa and I had fitted in with the other kids.

Then she related how she had come to hear of my father's death. She and her husband had been in Port Elizabeth at a youth event for the church. "Your parents were supposed to come with us that Saturday, but a few days beforehand your father told us they couldn't, because he had to be in King William's Town." In the middle of the service her husband had received a phone call. He called her aside and whispered the news.

"That was the end of the service for me," she said. "Oh my child, I really don't want to talk about Jijana! *Ebeyintonga yethu*. He was such a faithful man, one of our leading members."

What she told me next surprised me. My father had actually come to consult with the reverend and his wife before taking the job at the Peddie taxi rank. The offer had evidently thrown him into a quandary that tested his faith. My father knew only too well that the taxi industry was a harsh environment. He was well acquainted with its reputation for violence, greed and the temptation to run illicit side contracts. In the eyes of his church it was a veritable den of sin.

"We advised him against accepting the job," she told me.

But in the end my father decided that his obligation to his family came first. Work was work, he told them, and despite any qualms he might have had, he took up the offer.

Fortunately, Reverend Rhobo and his wife weren't people to force their views on others. So they let it go and gave my father their blessing. After all, the job offer had come from a fellow churchgoer.

I left Mam' uRhobo with a certain sadness, convinced that my father would have chosen any other way to make an income, if only he had had a choice.

Through the Legal Resources Centre in Grahamstown, I was put in touch with a forty-three-year-old prisoner, who I will call Mandisi,[*] in the hopes that he might share his insights into the taxi wars. Although he did not agree to be interviewed for this book, the synopsis of his life given by the legal representative gave me plenty to think about. How easily our paths might have crossed, I realised, had fate not dictated otherwise.

Mandisi was born in the Eastern Cape and his father was one of the few wealthy black people in the Ciskei in the 1960s. His family owned several general stores in small towns across the region, including one in my home village. But by the time I

---

[*] Not his real name

was born, the shop in my village had closed and Mandisi was living in another town. As a young man fresh from initiation and qualified as a maths teacher, Mandisi had decided to enter the taxi industry instead. He became a member of the Ncedo Taxi Association, the other major provincial association in our area and the arch-rival of my father's Bata. By the mid-1990s, Mandisi was rising through the ranks of Ncedo and had just been elected to the provincial taxi council.

When a province-wide taxi war with Bata broke out in 1996, Mandisi was ambushed twice and narrowly escaped with his life. As a result, he became involved in hit squads. He was at the centre of some infighting within Ncedo, and one day a friend of his was killed. The police showed up at his door the next day, and Mandisi was tried and sentenced to life imprisonment.

There was so much I would like to have asked Mandisi. What did he believe was the root cause of the taxi wars? What lessons had he learnt from his experiences? And why had he joined the taxi industry? Was it opportunity, the lack of constraints, the ease with which an astute taxi owner could make money?

Unlike my father, Mandisi was well educated and he wasn't poor. His first taxi van had been a gift from his father after his initiation.

Might I too have followed in my father's footsteps? Two cousins from my mother's side were taxi drivers, one of whose father was also a taxi driver.

Although my father had never actually asked me what I wanted to become, he loved us kids enough to accept that we would probably embark on a different life from his. But he must have realised that I was too timid and too lazy to survive the rough and tumble of the taxi rank. I also think he might have had higher hopes for me to do better than he had.

My father's own motivation for joining the taxi industry was clearly unemployment and the threat of poverty. But now that I had discovered the doubts that had plagued him before accepting the job, I started to think more deeply about his reasons.

After my uncle Xhantilomzi lost his farming job and began drinking, he never fully recovered. As a result, my father had become the man of the house. My father's own first-hand experience with alcohol might have especially motivated him, because the family now depended on him more than ever.

This situation probably influenced not just his choice to become a taxi driver, but also his earlier decision to join the church and become a responsible and disciplined man.

I think my father's conversion took place when he had hit rock bottom, and he saw religion as a way to rescue himself from his reckless lifestyle. Later perhaps, his faith might have waned, but by then the church had become his social circle.

Whether or not his faith ever waned, my father was certainly a very devoted man for a long time. In his diary he wrote:

A person that chose death because they see no future for themselves.

Further on he wrote:

> *Into ebangela umntu asokole ade afunukuzixhoma kungenxa yesono kodwa xa uthe wenza uxolo no-thixo wokufumana ukuphumla.*

This translates to "What makes a person so poor that they consider committing suicide is because of sin, but when you make peace with God you will receive peace from your troubles." It seems my father gave considerable thought to the experience of despair.

When I went away to university I drifted away from my parents' church. I didn't return to Christianity until many years later, when I too had hit rock bottom. In a fit of despondency, in the same year that I went searching for answers about my father's death, I also became a born-again Christian.

I had just gone through another hellish break-up with a girl and blown another job opportunity. I was suffering from constant fatigue. At the time I had no idea that this was one of the signs of the early stage of grieving. When I returned to my village, I felt like a great disappointment to my mother and myself, especially after having matriculated with flying colours.

The church promised me peace from my troubles, much as my father's church had done for him. Oddly enough, it was based far from Peddie in a little town called Qumbu deep in the former Transkei. An old high school friend was a member, and he looked really happy and said nice things about it.

The leader of this messianic church was educated, and had taken his cue from an American revival preacher from the 1950s, William Marion Branham. We had all the Branham paraphernalia – recorded talks, published sermons, even photographs. To display our piousness, all members were expected to hang one of Branham's poster-sized pictures in their homes. I didn't. Branham had called his church the Ministry of William Branham, and our leader occasionally called our church by this name. But mostly he insisted that the Bible never gave a name to the Christian church. It was just the church of God. A no-name church.

Our leader was a smarmy, bossy character who called himself Brother. He had a fondness for putting his hand on the waists of some of the younger "sisters" before inviting them to his house for sleepovers. Although he didn't like the young men in his congregation to have wives, he was suspiciously friendly with their wives. He claimed to be a modern-day prophet, so naturally there was a lot of screaming from the women – who made up two thirds of our small congregation. There were a few get-togethers where there was talk "in tongues", and visions that were really dreams, with women throwing themselves at him in fits of spiritual ecstasy. It was all done with such amazing grace.

Where was I in all of this? Right in there with my hands in the air, shirt as a damp as a *vadoek* as I screamed out hallelujahs.

As a journalist with a trained mind, I had started off asking questions, of course. But the leader cleverly conditioned us to believe his lies the minute we walked in, indoctrinating us with appropriate verses so that we would censor our awareness of any contradictions. We were forever urged to ask anything, but we were never answered truthfully, and were led to understand only what he wanted us to believe. So when people in the street raised the same questions with me, I had my answers all ready. It took me a year to catch on that we weren't as noble as we claimed to be.

It was only when I chanced upon an article about suppressed grief that I realised what my problem had been all along. It was as if I had been living in a dark room, and by sheer fortune I had stumbled on the light switch. I saw that it was just the trauma of my father's loss that had caused this spiritual hunger in me, and made me susceptible to the influence of this charlatan. In a sense my conversion was something of a wake-up call; a flashing red light warning me that I had issues I needed to face up to. And that's when I understood that writing about my father's story would help me to come to terms with the pain of my father's death in a healthier and more productive way.

Yet for a while it was wonderful – curative, even – to have licence to blame the Devil for all the battles I had faced and lost in my life. I had got so used to evoking the Devil's name for the tiniest setback that he became the scapegoat for all my anger and disappointment. My mother had always done the same. Once when my laptop fell off the table and the screen cracked, she said sadly, *"Usathana akayithandi into entle."* The Devil can't bear to see progress.

And there was also such value in the Christian teachings I was exposed to at this time, as my father too had discovered. I knew he had been especially moved by the Christian message of forgiveness, because in his diary he had written:

Father forgive them for knowing not what they are doing.

I believe he would have forgiven his killer. Yes, my father sometimes held grudges, even for a long time, but he never held them forever. He forgave when it was time to.

And very early in my quest I too decided to forgive whoever was responsible for his death. I knew that vengeful anger was not useful, and I couldn't allow resentment or malice to be my fuel. Even in the days immediately after my father was killed, despite feeling bereft and abandoned, I was mindful that taxi violence had claimed many others, not only my father.

Eighteen

AFTER FILING MY PAIA REQUEST, I continued to call the police every week to check the status of my application. Yet a niggling fear continued to taunt me. What if I was finally shown the docket? Would I really be able to cope with what it contained?

As the deadline for my Mampoer article drew steadily closer, my calls to the police intensified, and so did my anxiety. Finally, I received a response. I had been granted access to the police docket. It was with Captain Koedyk in East London's Organised Crime Unit, and he would be contacting me shortly.

Now I could no longer ignore my dilemma. In the PAIA application I had requested access to everything, including all photos of the crime scene. At the time I hadn't thought twice about ticking every box, in the journalistic conviction that there can be no such thing as too much information. I was determined to prise out every scrap of data about my father's murder – and photographs would allow me to verify the verbal accounts of my father's colleagues and the Bhikita man.

The problem was that in this case I wasn't just a journalist. And I had had more than enough problems with my emotions since my father's death. Was I sufficiently prepared to see his lifeless body in a pool of blood with a hole in his head?

By the time I spoke to Koedyk over the phone, I was open to any suggestion to avoid any gruesome images that might torment me whenever I closed my eyes. And to my great surprise, in spite of my anger and frustration at the behaviour of his colleagues and the delay with my application, he seemed genuinely interested in helping me. We came to an agreement that he would answer my questions fully from the information available in the docket.

But he made it clear upfront that any comments he had to offer were not for the media but for a relation of the victim. I needed to give him my father's official name, ID number and place of residence before he was prepared to talk to me. As I didn't have his ID to hand, he accepted the birth date. Then he first confirmed the case's particulars with me.

"Your father was killed on July 4, 2003, yes? At about 7:30 in the morning at the King William's Town taxi rank?"

"Yes," I agreed.

"All right," Koedyk said finally. "What do you want to know?"

"Tell me what the witnesses said," I asked him. And he did.

"After stones were thrown at the taxi minibus, some of the men who ran out of it went to the office of the taxi association forum, to find the man they thought was responsible for attacking them. From the statements, it appears that your father was one of this group, who then started assaulting the people at the taxi forum office with knobkerries and stones. Subsequent to this altercation, the man they blamed ran away. A shot was fired. It was meant for that man. It hit your father in the head, and he died as a result."

Politely I asked Koedyk to slow down.

"The shot was meant for whom?"

"It appears your father was involved in an altercation with some of the people."

A city away from Koedyk, on the other side of the line, I nodded my head dumbly.

"The shot was not for your father," he repeated. "It was meant for the guy running away in front of your father."

Despite the grenade Koedyk had just thrown me, my consciousness of being a journalist profoundly affected the direction and tone of my questioning. My next question was, "Did you establish who fired the shot? I mean, was it from my father's side or the other side?"

"It appears it was from somebody within the group of your father."

He was trying to cover the facts so quickly that I couldn't be sure of what I was hearing. I wanted to go back three questions and ask for more details, but the captain just kept on.

"Somebody was arrested, but the case was subsequently

withdrawn. An inquest was held and nobody was found to be responsible. The cartridge that was found at the scene could not be linked to any firearm."

For a second time, I appealed to Koedyk to slow down.

"Were you able to establish without any doubt that the person who killed my father was from the same group as him?"

He asked which taxi association my father had belonged to.

"Bata," I told him. "My father belonged to Bata."

"Bata, Bhikita, are they not the same?"

"No," I said and explained the difference. And because I was in no rush to conclude the interview – although Koedyk evidently was, as he had to get to court that morning – I steered him back to what he had said in the beginning.

"You said 7:30 am is the time my father died?

"The whole thing started at about seven o'clock."

"Was he the only person who died that morning?"

"Ja, he was the only one shot."

"You said there was an arrest?"

"Yes. But as I say, the case was withdrawn due to insufficient evidence."

Then Koedyk began to ask me questions of his own.

"Are Bata and Ncedo not the same?"

Again, I explained the differences.

He asked if I had spoken to Bata.

"I have," I said.

"What did they tell you," he wanted to know.

"They told me how he died. But I want to hear what the police have on the docket. The official account." Remembering his question about Ncedo, I asked, "Was the person who fired the shot from Ncedo?"

"The person who was arrested," the captain said, "and charged with the murder was from Ncedo."

This was a contradiction of what he had just said, Ncedo being one of Bata's competitors, not an ally, and certainly not on that morning in the same group as my father.

"How long did it take you to arrest the suspect?" I asked.

"The arrest was on July 10," the captain said. That was six days after my father was shot.

"When was he released?"

"The case was withdrawn on 20 January 2004 and the suspect was released."

At this point we discussed the justice system. The police had handed the docket to the Director of Public Prosecutions at the Grahamstown High Court, under which King William's Town falls, and an inquest was ordered. But after the inquest in King William's Town, the case wasn't pursued. I would have to be a lawyer to understand the reasoning.

"What weapon did the suspect use?"

Koedyk refused to give these specifics, because the suspect was released and presumed innocent. Giving such details would amount to accusing the wrong man.

I returned to my confusion about my father dying from a gun pointed by a Bata associate, when an Ncedo suspect was arrested for his murder.

He tried to clear up my concerns. According to the police and the witnesses they interviewed at the King William's Town taxi rank, the vehicle my father had been stationed in was ambushed by a group believed to be from the Bhikita-Ncedo taxi forum. My father jumped out along with Gwejela and the others of his group.

After my father broke away from his group and ran, the police believe he joined another group of Bata men.

My father and the other men were then engaged in a commotion. Everyone was out in the open getting up close and personal with one another, waving knobkerries and Okapis that they had hidden in nearby shops to bypass the police searches. Things were at boiling point by this time, and my father would have been very wound up. Then someone somewhere pulled out a gun.

When people heard the gunshot, some ran off shrieking, but others just stood and watched. Some witnesses claimed there were up to a hundred men in each group facing one another, all equally hostile and ready to fight.

"You father was killed by a comrade." This was the official story Koedyk was telling me.

Throughout our interview, I focussed on the article I would write, thinking I may be called upon to render every detail of my father's final moments or give vivid particulars of the crime scene. So I tried to extract as much detail as Koedyk could give me.

The captain said the cartridge found at the crime scene was from a handgun.

"How many bullets were found at the crime scene?"

"One."

"How far was it from my father?"

"Right next to him."

"Do you know where exactly he died at the rank?"

"Between the taxi forum offices and the toilets."

"How many witnesses did you interview?"

"About ten."

"What kind of people?"

"Taxi operators, hawkers, shop owners."

"When you say the suspect was released due to insufficient evidence, what do you mean?"

"This guy owned a firearm," Koedyk said, "and this firearm was found on him when the police arrived at the taxi rank and began searching everyone on sight."

"And did the bullet match his gun?"

"No, it didn't match."

He told me how the Director of Public Prosecutions, based at the High Court in Grahamstown, determines which cases end up in court, depending on whether certain requirements have been met and satisfactory evidence provided.

I asked for more information about the inquest. He explained that an inquest could be formal or informal. He couldn't say for sure what kind had been held in my father's case, but there was no sign of a subpoena. This indicated that it must have been informal – just a magistrate and a prosecutor going over the details without the suspect appearing in court.

I told Koedyk that I would mention his name in the story, and he reluctantly agreed.

I asked if there was still taxi violence going on today.

"No, no," he said. "It's over and done."

How had my father's case ended up with him, I wanted to know.

"I was in charge of the unit's taxi violence section at that time."

"So did you go to King William's Town to investigate that day?"

"Yes, I did."

"Then please describe the scene for me," I asked.

There was silence for a few seconds. Then he remarked on how many questions I had already asked. He was clearly starting to tire. But I took his complaint as a cue to explain my article and its objectives, which I did.

Koedyk said that the King William's Town police were naturally first on the scene. He and colleagues from the unit had driven through from East London, less than an hour away, as soon as they got the call.

"By the time we got there, it was a standstill."

"What happened after you arrived?"

"Your father's body was covered with a blanket," Koedyk said, "and then there was the post-mortem."

I asked about the entrance wound, and how long it would have taken my father to die.

"Less than a minute," he said.

Maybe I sounded a little too curious in an unhealthy way. "Why are you punishing yourself like this?" he asked.

I explained that I had always wanted to know these things. That every detail was important to me. That it was just good to know.

I should have said that I wasn't after revenge. But my answer seemed to satisfy him.

"It was just unfortunate. Your father was at the wrong place at the wrong time."

His words suddenly hit home. This is what I had failed to understand and accept over the years. My father was a taxi driver – he knew the job came with danger. He was killed on a vigil in King William's Town during which he well knew there could be violence.

"It was bad luck for your father," Koedyk continued. "It wasn't your normal taxi violence, where a gun battle breaks out and people get killed."

He reminded me that a weapons ban had been instituted at the taxi rank long before my father was killed. That was why, among all those people at the scene that morning, they found only one person with a gun on him. People were fighting with sticks and knobkerries, but one of them just happened to be carrying a gun.

"Unfortunately your father was taken out by his own group of people," he said. "That's it."

Nineteen

"Leave it there," said my mother.

I had paid her a visit to share what I had found out from the police. She took the news well, and as we sat together waiting for our food to cook, I knew she was right.

I was ready to let it go.

But having come to know the history that had made my father the man he was, I wanted to pay my respects to his grave and that of his father. I felt a deep need to connect to my bloodline. I still hadn't fully understood that by trying to know my father and my heritage, I was trying to know myself and my place in the world. If at any point I could have described my faith as being indigenous, this would have been the time. I wanted so badly to connect to my ancestors that I would have slaughtered a kraal full of cattle if necessary.

"There goes Nokhaya's son."

"Where's he going?"

"Who knows."

"He still hasn't graduated?"

"We would have heard if he had."

"*Hayi*, that young man."

This is what I imagined my village neighbours in Prudhoe were saying as I left my mother's home, passed the village sports ground. I took a familiar footpath, well known to all the young men of my village, who are required by custom to gather together and dig the grave whenever a local person has died. Taking my time, I walked up the little rise to the village cemetery at the top of a low hill. It was small, with a tree at the centre and a few tombstones and sinking crosses.

Below that of grandmother Nodabadini who had died in 2007, and uncle Xhantilomzi who had died in 2010, lay my father's grave. *In loving memory of our dear Fundisile. Remembered by family.*

I stood in silent contemplation for a long minute. There was a lot I wanted to convey to him, especially now that I understood him better, but I preferred silence. I felt I had come closer to reaching his spirit – to use the language of my ancestors – by visiting the crime scene in King William's Town where he had lost his life.

Resolving to return soon to tidy his grave and straighten his nameplate, I turned and made my way along the forest walk to kwaKerry. I could have taken a shorter route to *bawomkhulu* Magala's grave, but I chose the roundabout direction. The footpath led through closely packed trees – *umbhongisa*, *isiphingo*, *ncum-ncum* and *nontsholokothwane*. Gradually the forest gave way to *ipayindeshi* and knee-high grass. I remembered eating *intlaka* off the thorn trees as a boy. There were anthills to dodge. Sleepy-eyed cows munching their grass regarded me coolly. Then the path dipped to the sandy floor of a dry stream. After an hour I reached the gate of the farm fields, halfway up a hill.

The ground was freshly turned. It was the beginning of the farming season for many. In the distance I saw drinking wells, and an abandoned borehole as dry as a forgotten pot plant.

Bawomkhulu's grave, as I knew it, was off a dirt road, just beyond the farms. It was unmarked, except for a *naboom* tree that a cousin had remembered to plant beside it, since buying a gravestone was an unimaginable luxury for my grandfather's people.

In the distance a lagoon shimmered. Gangs of flies and noisy insects were whispering in my ears as I stopped to get my bearings. Ants climbed my shoes to explore the land inside my pants. As I neared the border of the farm fields, tractor tracks pointed the way to the road.

First I located the overgrown shrubs where the Jijana household – a mud rondavel and a one-room flat – had once stood, near the circle of oak trees that had sheltered the Cummings's household from the elements. The kraal had been in front of my family's household, and that was where my grandfather still lay.

I had twice visited his grave at the Cummings's farm in

the past two years, but those visits had been out of duty and self-interest. This time it was something more. I wanted a connection. A bond. Affection.

The first time I had forgotten to leave a mark, but on the second occasion I had left three small stones near the tree, as if to say, I had been here and paid my respects. And there they were.

I put down another three stones. Why three? Who knows. The number comes up a lot in my family. I am one of three siblings. My grandfather was also one of three. My father was one of three sons. And three of *bawomkhulu*'s family had now passed away – my grandmother, my uncle and my father.

As with my father, I realised, I had never got to know *bawomkhulu* Magala before his death. I knew that visiting his grave wouldn't solve anything, but it would make me feel better.

As I stood there, gazing at the grave, I felt better already. Gradually I grew aware of the grasshoppers, the twittering birds; the chorus of life all around me. At last I turned to retrace my footprints in the sand with a lighter step. I had never before felt so free.

"The past will always be a powerful presence in the present," says Zakes Mda. "But this does not mean that we must cling to the past ... only look back in the past in order to have a better understanding of our present."

Twenty

I BEGAN WRITING THIS STORY the day my father died. I say this because, much as you sometimes know from a stranger's eyes exactly what they are thinking, people could see that I was struggling long before I knew it myself. It is always hard to talk about what pains us the most – why else would I have had to construct imaginary interviews to express what I could not bring myself to say? How best to be able to unburden myself by telling my story of heartache was the question I had to solve.

How are you with your emotions now?

I'm like a recovering alcoholic. It gets easier every day. I feel like I've just got back from rehab and now I'm adjusting to life, trying to fit in.

Does your life feel different now?

Yes. I am grateful for this second chance. I laugh more easily. Every day I become more like my old self, my natural self. I feel kinder to people, I take life less seriously, I play with younger children. I'm no saint and I have my troubles, but I try to be a better person now to those around me. The last stage of the mourning process is sometimes called decathexis. It means giving some of your love for the deceased to the other people and things in your life. It means getting over your loss and thinking about the future. That's where I am now.

Have you found inner peace?

Nothing spiritual, but yes, I'm working towards peace of mind. I feel like I've come back to the community and it's my duty to be of value to society.

Has your feeling about death changed?

Let me answer you with the words of Nadine Gordimer. "If you ask 'What happens when we die? Why do we die?', you are asking 'Why do we live?' ... It's a turnabout business; it's your turn and then it's mine, and life is taken up by somebody else. Human beings are never reconciled to this ... If somebody dies young it's so terrible, it's such a tragedy, and the sense of waste is so strong; you think of all the promise that was there. And then if people live into old age, there's the horror of decay ... So it's the mere fact of death that we can't accept."

So what lesson have you taken away from this experience?

That you can't be too strong for too long. Tragedy is a part of life, and living a happy life after a tragedy requires accepting that life keeps changing, whether we like it or not.

We have to readjust when change happens, and let life go on. But sometimes we get so good at hiding our pain that we think we're over our tragedy. At that point, self-delusion becomes the tragedy.

Did learning about the circumstances of your father's death change anything for you?

Yes. At my father's funeral, Gwejela had told us that it wasn't my father's turn to be on duty that Friday that he died. He had been allocated the Saturday shift, but had switched places with a colleague the preceding week so he could have his Saturday free. I had forgotten all about this until I began the research for this book, when some of my father's colleagues reminded me. Strangely enough, it gave me a huge sense of relief. My cry of injustice about my father's murder – the thing that had always made it so hard to accept – was that it was so unnatural, so unnecessary. It was caused by a fight between taxi associations that could have been resolved by peaceful means. But that my father too had played a part in the events by choosing that particular shift underscored the fact that his death was a culmination of many, many factors. In the end no one could have stopped it. It was as if it had already been decided, and the sequence of events set in motion. So I could finally accept what my mother had always said.

It was his time to go.

Did you get everything you wanted from this quest?

I did.

What exactly had you wanted?

To know how my father had died. To know, not that he was a hero, but that like me, he was a survivor. To know that my father was a good man. That he loved himself and his family. That he did all he could to give his children a better life. That his spirit will remain with me forever.

And to see my father one last time in the driver's seat with my siblings and me beside him. To set out together on a Sunday evening to visit my mother in her quarters at the Mpekweni Resort. To see my father put on a gospel cassette to silence the grumble of the gravel as we speed towards the sea. To hear him hum along while my sister nearest to him sings the chorus. To see my little brother on my father's lap, holding the steering wheel and pretending to drive. To lean against the passenger window and drum out the tune on the dashboard, our seating arrangement comfortably reflecting our relative closeness to him.

To hear my father say in minor irritation, "Thabo, don't do that." To sink back with the secret relish a mischievous child takes from a reprimand. To hear my father say, "We'll leave you behind if you do that whenever I take you somewhere," knowing he never would.

To gaze in silence at the forest surrounding the car. To see the dusty road winding towards the sea, our speed so slow that already I'm beginning to miss home. To perk up as my mother's hotel comes into view, and watch for the turnoff to appear. To grow bored with the scenery and join in the singing as the road rises and falls through the forest.

To finally pull up at my mother's flat and jump out. To see my parents smile and exchange glad greetings. To watch my mother pick up my little brother and shower him with all the usual endearments.

To see my mother's smile before she suffered the worst. To see my father happy, before his ultimate sacrifice. To see the five of us together, a happy family in one room, beloved on this earth, when all we had was each other.

Acknowledgements

THIS BOOK WOULD NOT HAVE BEEN POSSIBLE without the help, patience and goodwill of a few people. Many thanks to:

Liana Meadon, Alexandra Dodd and the Mampoer team at Parktown Publishers, who, while I was in the process of writing the original article, were all very nice to me.

Margaret Renn of Wits Journalism, whose acts of kindness came at the right time in my life.

Derek Workman out in the Kalahari, who is always helpful – a comrade indeed.

Thabïso Mahlape, a kind soul and my publisher at Jacana Media, and Gwen Hewett, my editor.

My mother Nokhaya Jijana who gave her blessing early on.

My brother and sister, Sinovuyo and Thabisa Jijana, for serving as willing couriers, loan sharks and guiding angels.

And lastly, a song to my good friend, Nwabisa Ngumbela. Through you I know I have become a better human being.

Notes

1 The Reconstruction and Development Programme, or RDP, was the Mandela Administration's economic policy framework that set out to alleviate poverty and other socioeconomic problems. Over a million houses were built for the poor and previously disadvantaged at this time, and more than twenty years on, these small, tightly packed, multi-coloured homes are easily identifiable in black townships.
2 See "The Three Stages of Grief: An Overview" by Nancy Weitzman. Published in *www2.sunysuffolk.edu*. Ditto: "Living With An Empty Chair" by Roberta Temes. Second Edition, 1980.

3 The equivalent of the English nursery rhyme:
   Two little dickie birds sitting on a wall,
   One named Peter, one named Paul.
   Fly away Peter, fly away Paul.
   Come back Peter, come back Paul.
4 See *History In Action* by D.L. Davel, H.A. Schreuder and E. Engelbrecht. Second Edition, 1987.
5 See "Killer teen 'taught that men don't cry'" by Sandi Kwon Hoo. Published by Independent Online, May 15, 2014.
6 See "When a parent dies" by Masanda Peter. Published in *Move* magazine, 12 June 2013.
7 See address at the launch of the South African National Transport Academy by Sbu Ndebele, Minister of Transport, Bloemfontein, October 25, 2011.
8 See "From Low Intensity War to Mafia War: Taxi violence in South Africa (1987–2000)" by Jackie Dugard. Published in the Centre for the Study of Violence and Reconciliation's Violence and Transition Series, Vol. 4, May 2001. It also touches on how the chaos in the taxi industry was seen to supplement the apartheid government's broader destabilisation strategies in the run-up to the 1994 elections, by exacerbating tensions within black communities.
9 See "A Violent Legacy: The taxi industry and government at loggerheads" by Makubetse Sekhonyane and Jackie Dugard. Published in Crime Quarterly, No 10, 2004.
10 See address at the launch of the South African National Transport Academy by Sbu Ndebele, Minister of Transport, Bloemfontein, October 25, 2011.
11 From my own research:
   Solomon Mbona, the chairperson of the Bata-affiliated Port Elizabeth and District Taxi Association (PEDITA), told me:

"There will never be an end to taxi violence until government begins to regard us as [proper businessmen in a proper industry] and pays attention to our needs." By "our needs" Mbona was alluding to misgivings by the taxi industry in the Nelson Mandela Metro about the city's BRT system, which Mbona said the majority of his colleagues were yet to embrace.

In the run-up to the 2010 FIFA World Cup in South Africa, BRT buses in Port Elizabeth had to be escorted by police after municipal property had been looted and taxi operators went on strike. Nelson Mandela Bay taxi boss Melekile Hani, who was murdered in May 2010, was the chairperson of Bata and led the opposition to the city's BRT plans – seriously ironic given that Hani was a local municipal housing official. Attempts to introduce the BRT system in other cities was met with similar violent resistance by the taxi industry. Still, the BRT system remains government's attempt at transforming the industry. Customised in each of the major cities, from Cape Town's "MyCiTi" to Johannesburg's "Rea Vaya", the rollout began in 2009 in preparation for hosting the FIFA World Cup, and continues at a slow and irregular pace today. "We are still not sure that what the BRT promises will be good for all of us," Mbona said.

12 See report of violence between Bata and Bikita in *The Evening Post* newspaper, Port Elizabeth. Published on December 1, 1993: "Sporadic gunfire was heard, police vehicles and taxis were damaged and taxis set alight this morning following a string of incidents yesterday when a long simmering feud between the Border-King William's Town Taxi Association (Bikita) and the Border Alliance Taxi Association (Bata) spilled over into violence … the situation was extremely tense this morning as rival taxis lined the sides of the Alice-Dimbaza road, members of Bikita

on the South African side and Bata on the Ciskei side ... The violence ... erupted after an ongoing dispute between Bikita and Bata over Bata's refusal to move from the Cathcart Street taxi rank in King William's Town ... following the council's decision to favour a single fully-equipped taxi rank in the Market Square rather than the temporary rank ... The notice was ignored by Bata, whose deputy chairman, Kaizer Nanto, said the decision had been made without consulting Bata, and ... Bikita had been given too much power by the civics and the municipality."

13 See "Taxi violence claims 2 lives" at News24.com. Published January 8, 2014.

Taxi violence continues to rear its ugly head. Although the South African Police Service's Setati Phuthi told me the police do not collate statistics on taxi-related violence, media reports confirm that taxi violence silently rages on. In 2010, Port Elizabeth taxi boss Melekile Hani died in a hail of bullets while socialising in a township tavern, while prominent Tzaneen taxi mogul Risky Mobai was shot dead outside his mansion last year. By the end of April 2012, taxi violence had claimed over ten lives in the Mpumalanga Township outside Durban, in KwaZulu-Natal, with similar stories emerging from Pretoria East and Cape Town. And just this past February, a long rivalry between two of the Eastern Cape's major taxi alliances spilled over into neighbouring KZN, when two people were gunned down in Durban's CBD in broad daylight. In the midst of all the bloodletting, a *Sowetan* editorial complained, "Violence will continue unabated if the authorities do not take steps to regulate the taxi industry," echoing what a KZN MEC for transport, community safety and liaison, Willies Mchunu, is reported to have told the KZN cabinet: "We think it's high time we looked for extraordinary measures to address instability in the taxi industry."